R.A. Butler
An English Life

R.A. Butler

An English Life

Patrick Cosgrave

Quartet Books
London Melbourne New York

First published by Quartet Books Limited 1981
A member of the Namara Group
27/29 Goodge Street, London W1P 1FD

ISBN 0 7043 2258 7

Typeset by Trendsetter Photoset Ltd, Brentwood, Essex

Printed in Great Britain by The Anchor Press Ltd and bound by
Wm Brendon & Son Ltd, both of Tiptree Essex

This book is dedicated to the memory of Rosemary Marten with whom I worked so happily for several years, first in that home of the Butler heritage, the Conservative Research Department, and later on the *Spectator*. Despite her youth she was one of the finest exemplars of the Butler tradition in Conservative politics. She adorned everything she touched; she had greatness and sweetness of nature; and she lives, I believe, in the memory of everyone who knew her.

Contents

1
The Man

I first met R. A. Butler in 1970, after Edward Heath's triumph in the June election of that year. I was then working in the Conservative Research Department (CRD) in Old Queen Street, London, but I was living in Cambridge, where he was Master of Trinity, a post which gave him great satisfaction at the end of a long political life, and for which he had been recommended – the appointment of the Master having remained a royal prerogative – by Harold Wilson. The CRD, though not his creation, had waxed mightily under his benign influence just after the war and it seemed suitable to James Douglas, its then Director, that one of its officers should be seconded to help Butler prepare the first Swinton lecture, which he was to deliver at the Conservative College in Yorkshire which had been bequeathed for educational purposes to the party by Lord Swinton. Since I lived in Cambridge, and Butler came only irregularly to London, and since I had a Cambridge academic background, I was the obvious choice. Thus, for some weeks I visited him regularly and took copious notes of our meetings. Such was the impression that our series of meetings made upon me at the time that, though I have learned a great deal more about him (and, I hope, about British politics) in the succeeding years, I do not think my assessment of his character and achievements has changed more than marginally.

Right assessment of Butler's character, and the background which shaped it, is more than ordinarily crucial to any judgement of him. His political career, both as to duration, seniority and variety of appointments held, is rivalled in this century only by Churchill's. As Iain Macleod said, in rebuke of those who shared Harold Macmillan's opinion in 1963 that he had not the steel to be Prime Minister, he always did an unexpected or difficult job far better than anybody expected. And if today there are many able Tories sharply critical of his Education Act, his role in the wind-up of the Central African Federation, or his tenure of the Chancellorship of the Exchequer, then hindsight, I am sure, is one of the main features of their arguments. When he declined, in 1963, to fight Lord Home for the leadership of the party, and thus for the Prime Ministership, he commanded without effort the loyalty of men as diverse as Macleod and Enoch Powell, both of whom refused to serve his victorious rival.

This decision not to fight, because of the risk of splitting the party (there were, of course, no elections for the party leader in those days), hangs like a retrospective shadow over his whole career. It seemed to many at the time proof positive of the truth of Macmillan's criticism of him. Moreover, as details emerged of his – junior but not insignificant – role in the formulation and execution of the pre-war policy of appeasement; when his own autobiography mentioned Churchill's surprise at his eagerness to take on the Department of Education during the war, in preference to a more militarily active role; and when he himself confessed that he thought that he should have had the nerve to float the pound while he was Chancellor, a certain conviction about Rab's inherent flabbiness began to become current, at least among the more muscular-minded Tories. He said he would not fight Home, because he feared splitting the party he had served for so long, and it is certainly true that many on the Tory right had never forgiven him for his opposition to the Suez expedition in 1956. On the other hand, it is not in the nature of the Conservative Party to remain divided for long; and the right had suspected Harold Macmillan as well, for being both 'first in' and 'first out' at the time of Suez. For what it is worth I share the conviction Macleod expressed to me many times during the course of the 1970 campaign, when I worked closely with him, and which, I believe, Enoch Powell holds to this day, that had Butler stood by his guns in 1963 he would have been Prime Minister, the party would have rallied, and he would have won the 1964 election, shortly after the Conservative defeat after which he retreated to Trinity. These might-have-beens are, of course, of little real substance; the surprising thing about Home's career as Prime Minister is not that he lost in 1964, but that he so nearly won. The might-have-beens, however, are useful matters for thought when considering the life and career of one of the most elusive, ambiguous and capable figures in the history of British politics this century.

I had several reasons for being delighted with the Swinton assignment. I had been trained as an historian and here was an opportunity to meet and converse with one of the major politicians of the age, just at a point in his life when, no longer constrained by the responsibilities of office, he was still close enough to the past and even to great affairs to have a mind unclouded by false memory. He was, furthermore, reputed to be notoriously indiscreet – which would be a delight in itself – and he had a very strong academic bent, which might well incline him to kindliness towards a young man such as myself, working in politics, but struggling at the same time to complete a doctoral dissertation. I was not disappointed in any of my expectations, which is probably why it took so long to complete a by no means difficult lecture.

There was another more immediate, and possibly more powerful, reason for my enthusiasm. To me as a student, journalist and historian Butler was a major and fascinating figure of the relatively distant and the immediate past. But to me, as an officer in the Conservative Research Department (CRD), he was, because of what he had done to revive the department after the war, a living and powerful presence. It was not just that photographs of him hung in all sorts of odd corners in the department's two houses in Old Queen Street. Rosemary Marten, to whose memory this study is dedicated, Christopher Patten (subsequently Director of the department, and now the Conservative member for Bath) and I shared a room which had been used after the war by three of Old Queen Street's most distinguished graduates – Iain Macleod, Enoch Powell and Reginald Maudling – all of whom had been recruited by Butler. Across the corridor was our Head of Section, Charles Bellairs, a delightful father figure to us and one who, at the drop of a hat, would reminisce about the great days when, under Butler's guidance, the department had re-made the image of the Conservative Party after the shattering defeat of 1945. In retrospect I now question whether all of the programme of modernization was wise, and I fancy that Churchill simply used a good deal of it as window dressing. But at the time Charles Bellairs's stories were meat and drink to us youngsters, and the prospect of spending some time intimately working with the man at the centre of most of them was exceptionally enticing.

Nor was Charles Bellairs the only survivor of the old days in Old Queen Street. There were several others, among them James Douglas, whom I have already mentioned, and Miss Avis Lewis, the department's Establishment Officer since, it seemed, the flood. Miss Lewis had a photographic memory, not so much for the history of the department as for the people who had passed through it. All of them – officers, secretaries and politicians alike – seemed to her to be of an age, and though by no means every one of them gained (or retained) her affection, those who did were assured of staunch and valuable support in inter-office squabbles, and when they passed on to other things their doings were followed with minute and loving attention. For Butler she had a particular fondness, which she did not extend to his successor as Chairman of the department, Michael Fraser (now Lord Fraser of Glenmorack). The reason for this was simple. Miss Lewis kept a succession of bull mastiffs, giant, but notoriously short-lived, dogs. The current mastiff came to the office every day, and dozed the working hours away in her room. To be on good terms with Miss Lewis it was essential to enjoy at least good diplomatic relations with the current dog. Michael Fraser was always a trifle nervous of the great beasts but Butler, I was told, besides extending to Miss Lewis the courtesy of a visit and a friendly chat whenever he came to the office, enjoyed superlative relations with her canine companions. The conversations I had with such old colleagues as Avis Lewis and Charles Bellairs gave me, long before I met him, insight into and evidence of Butler's exceptional ability to attract and hold the personal loyalty of very disparate individuals, a powerful trait which became widely recognized only after the crisis of 1963 was over.

I am still by no means sure that I can pin down what there was – and is – about his personality that produced this magnetism. He is not, and never has been, a physically appealing man. Throughout his career he has been dogged by the distrust of many colleagues because of his taste for evasiveness and ambiguity, especially in conversation, or when relating some of his more dismissive and even contemptuous anecdotes about former colleagues. His air of effortless intellectual superiority has maddened many throughout the years; yet very few of the Butler loyalists are equal to him in intellect and there are fewer still who have not, at some time, felt the edge of his tongue. At a private Cambridge dinner in 1969, for example, when the guest of honour was Edward Heath, Butler, in the chair, made an extremely witty and rather donnish little speech of introduction which stopped barely short of being openly insulting, not only to the leader of the party but to many of those still prominent in its affairs who had been not colleagues, merely, but friends, including Macleod, Powell and Maudling. It remains a puzzle to many, moreover, that a man possessed of so powerful, cutting and ruthless a tongue should in action so often have been seized by a fit of indecisiveness.

The wit – and it is essentially not only a private wit but an obscure and academic one – has rarely issued in powerful public pronouncements. Butler has always taken exceptional care with the preparation of his speeches, but they have almost always seemed flat. In the opening passages of his delightful book *The Life of Politics* Henry Fairlie (to whom Butler was and is a hero) gives a fascinating account of a speech by Butler to a hostile Tory conference on the subject of capital punishment, to which he was opposed, but which the conference rabidly supported. He won the vote, but only after a speech of almost impenetrable obscurity and resolute lack of life which both confused and numbed his audience. Thus he cannot be said ever to have possessed that public charisma which, in compensating for private deficiencies, could explain the powerful loyalties he has always excited.

I suspect that one of the principal reasons for Butler's success in acquiring and retaining loyalty is his capacity as a teacher, and that, too, is best illustrated by his influence on the CRD. That department has always enjoyed special favour and influence within the party. It has been well-endowed – spectacularly so in comparison to its Labour equivalent, though Labour is supposed to be the intellectual and the Tory Party the non- or even anti-intellectual party. Good management over the years has ensured that, while there is a steady stream of gifted young men and women in and out, there remains a hard core of able, but older, administrators *in situ*. Almost all of them I have met or worked with – and this, I believe, is especially a heritage from Butler – do not simply see their task as restraining hot-headed, radical and ebullient youth, but in encouraging it, and drawing it out, widening its experience and deepening its perceptions. It is not without significance that most of those who have served at the CRD refer to themselves as graduates, and while there is little of the formal about the nexus of such graduates, intimacy between them is usually easily renewed, even after long passages of time. When I worked there, especially before the 1970 election, when the department was unusually large and under the guidance of a particularly gifted Director, Brendon Sewill, we had instilled in us a high sense of corporate loyalty, and we were made aware of the fact that application and originality were constantly required. And we were made particularly aware that that was the way Lord Butler – who by then had no connection whatever with us – liked things done. I am not sure that that tradition is as strong now as it was in the late 1960s, but when, on economic grounds, the decision was taken in 1979 to move the CRD into Central Office in Smith Square, a quite substantial number of the graduates protested, often bitterly, that this amalgamation with the far larger and more impersonal structure of Conservative Central Office would weaken the department and destroy its Butlerian traditions. The fact that the dominant faction in the party had members increasingly suspicious of, and even hostile to, the Butler legacy did nothing to allay such fears.

It is hard to exaggerate the effect so zealously nurtured a tradition can have on young minds. For those not wanting to make a career there the department has the vital function of serving as a sort of post-university finishing school, and even served, I believe, a similar function for the young men who came back from the war in 1945. It was, and is, a function of adjustment, or readjustment of the balance between intellectual preoccupation and the politics of real – parliamentary – life. Before the war the department had two separate sections: one served the day-to-day briefing needs of MPs; the other concentrated on longer-term policy making. Butler, in his capacity as Chairman of the department, merged the two sections so the officer in charge of, let us say, Home Office affairs had both the task of dealing with a flood of mundane day-to-day questions from members and candidates (and briefing every Tory member for debates on his subject) and working in the higher regions of longer-term policy. The one task kept his feet on the ground; the other let him exercise his intellect. American political researchers are, in terms of financial endowment, even more superior to the CRD than the CRD is to the Labour Party's Research Department. But I think it fair to say that I have never, in spite of a wide and varied academic experience, seen so steadily excellent a stream of work as emanated from comparatively inexperienced young men and women in Old Queen Street in the 1960s. And most of this was due, not just to Sewill's capacity in picking and motivating his officers but, originally, to the reorganization that Butler put in train. By the time he went to Trinity he was too old, and possibly too tired, to make a significant impact on so large and entrenched an institution. But, had he chosen an academic career earlier in life, he would undoubtedly have made a superb teacher, and a great Head of House.

The pedagogic aspect of his character which I have

stressed in an institutional sense is often reflected in his longer conversations. He is fond of quoting a maxim of Talleyrand on the ideal conversation of the ideal Foreign Minister. Talleyrand, that great French Machiavellian, says the Minister's conversation 'must be simple, varied, unexpected, always natural and sometimes naif'. Butler believes that his conversation 'corresponds tolerably well to Talleyrand's requirements'. I would not say it is simple exactly, but every one of the other adjectives is devastatingly appropriate. It might appear surprising that I should accept 'naif' when I have already described the man as subtle, evasive and ambiguous. But it is a fact that he will frequently insert into an otherwise complex and complicated discussion an observation of almost startling banality, or a question of unutterable naïvety, amounting almost to childishness. In the middle of a discussion I once had with him on his time at the Home Office, for example – a period of which he is exceptionally proud – he suddenly stopped and asked: 'You did know I was Home Secretary once, did you not?' While I was gathering suddenly scattered wits to find the correct formal and appreciative reply to what seemed a silly and off-putting question he continued: 'And very good I was, too.' He then resumed the winding thread of his original discourse.

We see here, I think, not so much genuine naïvety or childishness as a natural attribute of what is in truth a highly combative mode of conversation. Butler delights to startle, and he will use whatever means come to hand to achieve that effect. His natural discourse is rambling, discursive and apparently without method, but shot through with insight, candour, anecdote and allusion. However hard it may be on subsequent reflection to divine his real or steadfast meaning, or to decide, even, where he meant to place the emphases while you were with him, and particularly if the talk was a lengthy one, you have the full impression of having been admitted instantly to a rare treasure house of a mind. Even if one merely meets him at a party and pauses to pay one's respects, spending perhaps no more than a few minutes in his company, he has, even if what he says may be simply baffling, obscure or just bitchy, the faculty of communicating both power of mind and intimacy of feeling. It is, I think, later reflection on the real meaning of what he said, and the frequent realization then that it was either ambiguous or unkind, that has earned him so many enemies over the years.

Paradoxically, his wit, like his conversation, is self-sufficient. If his interlocutor does not get the joke, the reference, or the point, Butler is still happy that a good one has been made. This self-sufficiency is physical as well as intellectual. Whenever I called on him at Trinity I would find him looking out of his window over Great Court, one of the finest (as he says himself) domestic spectacles in Cambridge. He would turn slowly as I came in, a large, rumpled figure with that ravaged battlefield of a face, the right hand (smashed in a childhood riding accident in India) folded in against his stomach. He would greet me, gesture to a chair on the right-hand side of his desk and proceed ahead of me to sit behind the festoon of photographs which covered his working surface. As often as not he would begin by talking about Tolstoy and the art of autobiography – a special matter for him, and the subject of his 1967 Romanes lecture, 'The difficult art of autobiography'. However friendly he was, he still invariably seemed both physically and intellectually remote.

He is nevertheless ever courteous and even gracious. He will sometimes (though not always) make almost a visible effort to avoid making a remark or a witticism which is hurtful either to the person he is with, or to somebody that person might know. He seems to hesitate before the fence of his own capacity devastatingly to summarize character or ability. But one feels the effort being made to restrain himself. One feels that it tires him *not* to be entertaining.

He will, if his mind is bent on being polite, sanitize some of his racier stories for the benefit of his audience, He reminds me, in these conscientious moods, of the great third Marquis of Salisbury (Prime Minister for longer than Gladstone) whose daughter, Gwendolen, tells us that he hated having to make speeches when he was tired, not because he feared he might be boring, but because he knew he would be entertaining.

These characteristics – and, so to speak, the flavour of this strange man – may be summarized by a brief account of Butler on Eden. Oddly enough, though Harold Macmillan beat him to the job of Prime Minister in 1957, set himself resolutely to the subsequent task of ensuring that Butler never got that job, and intrigued against him with great success in 1963, I have never heard him being cruel about Macmillan. He has been hostile: of Macmillan's multi-volume account of his own life, Butler once said, 'Harold tells me that the rule of autobiography is to tell the truth, the whole truth and anything but the truth.' But in spite of the fact that, as Iain Macleod said, 'The truth is that at all times, from the first day of his premiership to the last, Macmillan was determined that Butler, although incomparably the best qualified of the contenders, should not succeed him,' Butler has never sought to be unkind to, or to hurt, his great rival.

Eden is a different matter. Wilfred Sendall, the former political editor of the *Daily Express*, recalls a lobby conference – a meeting at which ministers and shadow ministers speak, entirely off the record, to journalists – which gave him a front-page story. Butler's celebrated remark about Eden – 'He's the best Prime Minister we've got' – had been widely quoted and reporters pressed him to say what he really thought about his chief. Butler, keen to get on to other subjects, shrugged and said, 'Oh, *capax imperii* and all that.' Sendall, alone among those present, could complete the quotation, *capax imperii nil nisi imperasset*, which might roughly be translated as, apparently capable to govern until called upon to do so. He was thus able to make a major story out of the implication that at least one of his senior ministers had no faith in Eden. Butler was amused.

In his own autobiography, *The Art of the Possible*, Butler says of Eden:

> Anthony's own temperament was a mixture of the charm of his mother and the artistic impetuosity of his father; the combination gave him a particular talent for sharp perspicacity in negotiations which culminated in his success in Indo-China in 1954.

I have, however, heard Butler relating these bland, and even gracious words in a quite different way. I was anxious to check out some of his more famous 'Rabbisms' with the man himself. I asked him if he had really ever said that Eden was 'the best Prime Minister we've got'. As soon as I had left him I wrote down his reply: 'Oh. I've said much worse than that. You see, Anthony's father was a mad baronet and his mother a very beautiful woman. That's Anthony – half mad baronet, half beautiful woman.' When I first read *The Art of the Possible* I was struck by the curious symmetry between the words he used in private. One can almost feel the artistry that has been used to tidy up a personal belief. The same elements, Eden's parents, are there, but those elements are brought into an entirely different relationship in the judgement for public consumption.

However, Eden was a rival. He was also a man for whose judgement Butler had no respect: I believe, indeed, that Butler had a certain, and not unmerited, belief that not only should he have been made Prime Minister in 1963 (over Home), and in 1957 (over Macmillan) but also that he should have succeeded Churchill, instead of Eden. He had, and has, no cause to love Eden. Enoch Powell, on the other hand, is a different matter. Powell was one of

Butler's early recruits to the post-war CRD. He was almost an acolyte; and he refused to serve under Home in 1963. Butler says of Powell: '...he was probably the most intellectually formidable of the men who have passed through the Research Department'. But:

> I remember that on one occasion he brought me a paper in which he argued that with ten divisions we could reconquer India. At his request I submitted the paper to Churchill, who seemed distressed and asked me if I thought Powell was 'all right'.

I have more than once heard Butler give a rather different account of the same occasion. Again, the materials used to form the judgement implicit in the anecdote are the same; but the artist has used his brush to coarsen, to emphasize and in other ways to alter their relationship to one another. Thus, in the conversational version, Churchill did not ask if Powell was 'all right', but if he was 'all there'. He says not just that he presented Powell's paper to Churchill, but that he took Powell to see the great man in his flat at Hyde Park Gate. (I am reasonably certain that this meeting never took place.) He says that, Powell having expounded his argument about India, Churchill and he left the younger man alone, whereupon Churchill grinned and said, 'Will you take him home or shall I?'

Reviewing *The Art of the Possible* Powell said: 'Lord Butler's memoirs are in a class by themselves. In literary distinction, choiceness of expression, polish and balance, they make the rest look botchwork.' And he concludes: 'They are also a work of astonishing self revelation.' That is no more than the simple truth. Unlike, say, the memoirs of Churchill, de Gaulle, Macmillan or Eden himself there is no posturing or obvious dramatization in *The Art of the Possible*. Indeed, Butler aimed a barb at his celebrated rivals in his preface: 'I have eschewed the current autobiographical fondness for multi-volume histories, and have preferred a single book that is not too heavy for anyone to hold up and doze over in bed.'

The book is direct, revealing and very personal. It is not short in its judgement on men and events, but above all one can feel through its pages the man himself in a way that is not possible in any other modern autobiography by a major political figure. Still, there remains the fact that, even without dramatizing, he has changed the whole colour and complexion of his beliefs and views in giving the public his view of his own life. It is true that he has threatened to rewrite the whole book and to tell, this time, the whole and unvarnished truth, but I doubt very much if that threat will ever be implemented. The mask has become the man, a man who, as Brendan Bracken wrote to Beaverbrook (during the 1957 succession crisis) 'is a curious blend of Gandhi and Boss Tweed'.

2
The Butlers and India

For all that he came so close to being Prime Minister Butler never seems to have regretted very much that the prize never fell to him. Even in moments of high political drama there has always been an element of the detached artist about him. In 1953, for example, when the political world was waiting with bated breath for Churchill to retire and for Eden to succeed, when Butler – because of Churchill's physical decline and Eden's constantly recurring ill-health – was bearing an enormous burden of governmental work, Lord Moran found him debating with Churchill the relative merits of Burke's and Macaulay's prose style. 'He seems none the worse', Moran observed, 'for the grind while the P.M. and Anthony were away ill. He does not get worked up like Anthony.' And later in the year, when Churchill's oft-postponed retirement did seem to be imminent Moran noted:

> It appears that Rab Butler is sitting on the fence with one leg dangling on each side. He likes cricket similes.

He is trying to keep a straight bat, he says. He is not trying to make runs.

Nevertheless, Butler, who has held every major office in government except the premiership, speaks and writes with unfeigned and deep nostalgia about one job which he – the word is not too strong – lusted after and never attained. 'If there is one long-standing political ambition whose non-fulfilment can still give me the sharpest of pangs,' he wrote, 'it is that I never became Viceroy.' It is hard, in the 1980s, to understand, and even harder emotionally and spiritually to appreciate, the driving force of that ambition, and the extraordinary fascination which the Indian subcontinent exercised over some of the best British political minds of the pre-war period. It is interesting to remark, however, that Butler is not alone among politicians, who came to the front of affairs after 1945, in having the singular and specific ambition of ruling India as Viceroy: Enoch Powell entered politics for the specific purpose of saving the Indian Empire, and avows to this day that his greatest dream was exactly the same as that of Butler. One can see, of course, the simple delight it would be possible to enjoy in ruling so vast and various a country with such a measure of independence from London as the greater Viceroys enjoyed: it was said of Lord Curzon, when he was Viceroy, that he treated with the home government not merely as an appointee, but as an independent power. But the fascination for such men as Butler and Powell lay, I believe, not so much in grandeur and power as in the nature of India itself, and in the idea of doing service to its many and conflicting races. In so far as it can be defined this fascination is, however, more a phenomenon of attraction to the Hindu than to the Moslem culture. Of the Butler family move from Rajputana to Lahore in 1909 Butler writes, with nostalgia, 'Here there was no dust, no dancing horses, no hyenas running near the camp in the early morning. India draw back a little and only came near if we went to the camel area ...' What has become Pakistan exercised little power over the young Butler, seven years of age when the move took place.

Powell,with the intensity and enthusiasm which is characteristic of him, fell in love with India during the war. Butler, on the other hand, had the Indian tradition bred into him: the tradition of service in the subcontinent was already two generations old on his mother's side when he was born. His father and his uncle both became governors of Indian provinces. During the years of the First World War – Butler was eleven at its outbreak – he and his sisters regularly dined with Indian princes serving in the war or supporting the war effort, at his uncle's London home. 'What is enduring', he wrote, 'is that we children ever after regarded Indians, and by extension all coloured people, as friends.'

Churchill had the same preoccupation. It is too readily forgotten today, when the principal element in the public memory of his career before 1939 is that of his role as the prophet of war, that Churchill spent most of his time in the later 1920s and in the 1930s arguing against the moves of the Baldwin and Macdonald governments towards Indian independence. It was on Churchill, indeed, that Butler cut his ministerial teeth in defending, as a junior minister, governmental policy on India. But Churchill knew India as a young subaltern: his account of his Indian experiences in *My Early Life* is probably the finest prose he ever wrote. However, unlike Butler, he did not have the experience of genuinely mixing with the Indians. In the case of the Butler family this intimacy was far more marked, and far closer, than was normal for Britons working in the Indian Civil Service. 'We did not have', Butler wrote, 'an Indian enclosed childhood such as Kipling describes in *Something of Myself*.' It was not, indeed, until the move to Lahore that the Butler children led anything like the common life of youngsters in their station – suburban and segregated from the natives. It thus followed that, unlike Churchill, Butler had an instinctive and unforced sympathy for the movement towards Indian independence. 'We were never infected', he says, 'with the Memsahib complex of "keeping them in their place".' And again: 'My time as a small child in Kotah made me sympathetic by instinct and in my innermost being when in later life the Indians were seen to seek and expect self-government.' In the circumstances, and given his background and feeling, it was a somewhat bizarre act on Butler's part even to forward to Churchill Powell's proposal for the reconquest of India. I suspect, however, that he may have had a mischievous intention in doing so.

It is important to remember, of course, that Butler left India when he was a small child, in pursuit of the unbending rule that Indian Civil Service children returned home to school. Nevertheless, there can be no doubt that the mark the place made on him was permanent. It may even, to some extent, explain the later rivalry with Macmillan. Many believe that Macmillan's obdurate opposition to Butler's succession in 1963 stemmed either from Butler's involvement with the pre-war policy of appeasement, or from his attitude to the Suez expedition. However, the late George Hutchinson, in his study of Macmillan, *The Last Edwardian at No. 10*, makes the shrewd point that Macmillan, thinking of Butler strictly as a contemporary, distrusted him because he had not shared the experience of the First World War. This was impossible, since Butler was only eleven years of age in 1914; and, as it happens, he speaks and writes with great feeling of the generation engaged in that ferocious struggle. To Macmillan, however, the war was *the* experience of his life, as India was to Butler. For all their work together in government over a generation, the two men had been cast in quite different moulds and, as Butler's luck had it, the advantages in their rivalry invariably fell to Macmillan.

It was not the fashion, during Butler's childhood, for children of his social class to mix a great deal with their parents. In this, however, as in other things, his parents were exceptions to the rule, at least until the time came for the children to return to England to school. It was Butler's father who gave him, at an early stage, the distinctive nickname 'Rab' – on the grounds, apparently, that it *was* distinctive, and would thus be helpful later when, as his father fully expected, the child would enter politics. But the father, though a loving and interested parent, was a very busy man, the major part of whose work consisted of lengthy treks across the Indian countryside to dispense justice, settle disputes and do his bit to ensure the smooth running of the vast machine of Indian Empire. Again unusually, at least until the removal to Lahore, the Butlers took their children on trek with them, and it thus came about that, young though he was when he left India for home, Butler was given an unusually thorough grounding in the characteristics and complexities of Indian culture and politics. To this day he speaks and writes movingly of these early days:

> The work entailed camping throughout the cold weather, moving from village to village to assess the land. We all went to camp, with a train of camels carrying tents, furniture and crockery. My sister Iris and I travelled in a cart pulled by two ponies called Peter and Polly; our parents rode everywhere and sometimes changed to elephant transport for crossing rivers. The tents were pitched by a grove of trees and we were let loose to wander in and out of tent-ropes and to climb the tent sides and slide down them. We went quite near the table placed by the office where father sat to receive petitions and give judgement and settle quarrels. Thus we witnessed the grass roots of government. Before

> sunset, the parents took a ride round looking at crops and land boundaries. In the very early morning, when the sun rose in a pink blaze over some huge plains, we were taken from our beds, wrapped in dressing gowns, and bundled into the cart to drowse till the breakfast stop, where we all paused to eat and dress properly till the camel train caught up with us. I remember the unfenced fields stretching away endlessly, dwarfing my puny gaze, and little realised that I would for many years (thirty-six in all) live and breathe in the wide spaces of the wheat fields of Saffron Walden.

The comparison between India and his constituency of Saffron Walden is, perhaps, a rather far-fetched one. But Butler has an unusually strong sense of place, especially unusual in a man of his ironic and detached temperament. In his memoirs he writes, for example, with great sweetness about his constituency, where for many years he and his two successive wives made their home, but it was India, it is clear, that made the deepest impression on his sensitive and absorbing mind.

Potent though the influence and example of his father was, however, it was clearly his mother who played the major part in forming the character and temperament of the young Butler; in this, if in no other respect, he was like Eden. I have never heard him being very precise in describing her crucial influence, but on all the evidence of those who knew her she was a woman of singularly sweet disposition. Perhaps her greatest gift to her son was the provision of an all-embracing love which created for him both an impenetrable security and a complete self-sufficiency: in this she seems to have been very like both of his wives, Sydney and Mollie Courtauld. Lady Butler (Mollie Courtauld), however, is possessed of a far more combative temperament than either his mother or Sydney Courtauld, as was witnessed in 1963 by her fierce determination that her husband should refuse to serve under Lord Home.

Lord Dunboyne, who has made a study of the Butler family genealogy, has argued that it stems, however remotely, from the Irish Butlers, a vast, originally Norman clan which, especially in the sixteenth and seventeenth centuries, lived a curious and powerful life halfway between native Irish and English settlers and whose most notable historical figure was the seventeenth-century James, first Duke of Ormonde. Butler is rather pleased with this implication of a wild and somewhat romantic Celtic background, and says that when he received his title he took the name of his constituency principally in order to distinguish himself from the Irish Butlers. There is, however, nothing remotely Celtic about him, though he might claim a more plausible Celtic ancestry than the Irish from his grandmother's close family connections with Cornwall. The truth of the matter is that, not least in its Indian connections, Butler's whole character and background are fundamentally, specifically and unalterably English – and English of a very special kind.

On his father's side the Butler record was impeccably an academic one. In 1794 his great-grandfather was Senior Wrangler at Cambridge and a Fellow of Sydney Sussex; Butler himself gave up a Fellowship at Corpus in order to enter politics. The great-uncle, Montagu, became both Headmaster at Harrow and Master of Trinity, a predecessor of Butler himself at that job. His father – also Montagu – became Master of Pembroke on retirement. Butler himself says that his life was, like the Cambridge examination, a tripos, composed of politics, Cambridge, and India. Iain Macleod used to say that 'Rab loves being a politician among academics and an academic among politicians; that is why neither breed of man likes him all that much.' Harold Wilson says that he offered to recommend Butler for the Mastership at Trinity, not merely in order to tease Alec Home (though that intention, he allows, was there) but 'to please Rab, who is a nice fellow and would feel that he had at least matched up to his family's expectations'. Butler celebrated that appointment by a book review in the *Sunday Telegraph* on Horace which managed to twist that Latin poet's gentle verse into a defence of Neville Chamberlain's pre-war policy of appeasement.

We have, therefore, a family (and Butler is exceptionally conscious, as Harold Wilson was aware, of family tradition) intimately connected both with India and with an ideal of academic excellence, though not one of them was a genuinely creative scholar. It was a family, moreover, imbued with the ideal of intellectual excellence as service. It was a family convinced that every academic attainment should be laid at the foot of the public weal – a Victorian tradition more usually associated with Oxford than Cambridge. Butler, who himself has read the classics principally in translation, and hints that they taught him less about politics and public service than did the speeches of the younger Pitt, none the less avers that the fact that his father was a classical scholar made him a superb Indian administrator.

It is not certain – and on the subject Butler is characteristically opaque – when he decided to go into elective politics. He claims that 'such political abilities as I have' came from his grandmother's side of the family, though his uncle Geoffrey sat in the House of Commons for Cambridge University and wrote a book about the philosophy of Toryism which Butler has lovingly edited. But he had certainly made that decision in his teenage years; and not altogether without family opposition. His approach to what became most of his life's work was characteristically stately: in 1926, at the age of twenty-three, he married Sydney Courtauld (who died in 1954, five years after which he married her cousin Mollie, the present Lady Butler) and went on a world tour, including his beloved India, before settling down to be the member for Saffron

Walden for thirty-six years. But all the time the thread of his career was based on the principle of using his exceptional brain in the service of the public good. To him the public good consisted from the beginning not merely in service to the people of this island, but to the people of the Empire; it was thus particularly hard for him, as Home Secretary, to introduce the first act controlling immigration into Britain. That combination which he has constantly exhibited, of academic excellence and devotion to the common weal, defined in an imperial and not just a British context, is something very specially and uniquely English.

It is also, however, worthy and admirable though it is, a submissive tradition, requiring not merely service, but silence, eschewing ambition for its own sake. Churchill said once that every man in politics was greedy, not just for sordid ends, but for fame. Such a concept was, and is, wholly foreign to Butler. But its very absence from his make-up has meant that, in all the great crises of his life, from appeasement to the battle of 1963, he has preferred the dust to the palm. Quite unlike Churchill, he almost glories in the submissiveness of his life, even observing of the moment when he entered Parliament that he 'proceeded to obey the instructions of the Conservative Chief Whip ...' And he was, for so intellectually self-confident and even arrogant a man, a superbly devoted constituency member for all his thirty-six years.

Acquiring a parliamentary nomination, especially for a young man with his connections, was not difficult for Butler. He had the advantage of being comfortably off; and his wife was wealthy. There is no doubt that he married for love – he had known Sydney for some time before their engagement – but the link with the Courtaulds was of considerable political help to him. His only tiny difficulty was a certain suspicion of his attachment to her daughter by his mother-in-law. This, Butler says, he overcame because he was a member of the Carlton Club and because, when carving, he could make a partridge do six. In any event, shortly after his marriage, he resigned his Fellowship at Corpus and embarked on a world tour, content to make his approach to politics in a leisurely fashion, and supremely self-confident that a Conservative nomination would duly come his way, his ambition for one being now widely known among his family connections. He was right: when the touring couple arrived in British Columbia they found awaiting them a letter from William Courtauld (Sydney's cousin) suggesting that Butler should put his name forward for Saffron Walden, the sitting member for which planned to retire. Courtauld added that the family would, of course, support their new in-law. Butler was duly nominated.

Though then safely Tory, Saffron Walden had been a Liberal seat and there remained, as Butler says, a strong radical streak among its constituents, as well as a more than ordinary predisposition to attend to the personal characteristics of the member. According to various memories of the time, there was more than a little doubt about Butler's suitability as a candidate, in spite of the powerful backing he enjoyed. He was very young. He seemed rather over-academic. Married as he was to a wealthy wife he would find it difficult, some Conservative Association officers felt, to establish an easy relationship with a basically agricultural constituency. P. A. Hunt, Butler's first agent, was the son of a publican and, though undoubtedly totally loyal – in the great tradition of Conservative agents – could be pardoned for having some initial reservations about the candidate. There was another point: though nearly all Conservative constituency organizations have generally been regarded, especially by their opponents, as exceptionally efficient, Saffron Walden was exceptional even by Tory standards. Would Butler, the question was asked, with his donnish manner and reserved ambiguity of personality simply prefer to rest on the laurels won by his predecessor rather than set out to win his own spurs?

All reservations and doubts were dissipated as quickly as they had been formed. Butler approached his task with an assiduity and an energy that were formidable. Every one of the hundred or more centres of population in the constituency, towns, villages and hamlets, was systematically canvassed. Rather than repeat current domestic political propaganda he showed – two or three times a night in different villages – a film he and his wife had made of the Indian part of their world tour. Local and national politics intruded only when, after meetings, the grievances of constituents were written down in the candidate's master volume of problems; they were subsequently dealt with with dispatch. To the amazement of his agent Butler fitted in happily in the local pubs – points of adjournment after the meetings – and supped beer with the natives. (Although, as he subsequently recorded, he stood as few rounds as possible. He observes, 'It is a great mistake for candidates, even years away from an election, to go into a pub and offer drinks all round immediately. It is better to receive half a pint than to give twenty.')

Some who recall those early days say it was not so much that Butler learned the ropes of constituency management quickly. It seemed, rather, that he came to his candidacy already fully equipped and able, indeed, to teach the experienced locals more than a trick or two. He had a feel for rural politics, and for simple people and problems, greater than any he was ever to show for the great game at national level. His speeches and his conversation were alike straightforward, unambiguous and unaffected. And, of course, the practical service he gave his constituents had no superior in the country, complaints and requests being dealt with to almost everybody's satisfaction throughout the thirty-six years of his holding the seat. As he started, so Butler went on.

The obsessive thoroughness which some at least of Butler's constituency officers were surprised to find in their young candidate is, indeed, a fundamental characteristic of his personality. Within a year of being nominated he knew every lane and by-way in Saffron Walden, and to the end he could correct experienced ministerial drivers on the routes through the constituency. If he did not have warmth or ebullience of personality his very devotion to their interests and their place won him devoted support among all classes: it was the drovers from the cattle market who carried him in triumph on their shoulders from the Town Hall to the Conservative Club on the night of his election in 1929.

There must have been nevertheless a certain amount of strain for him, over the years, in bending to the demands of colleagues who, in his opinion, were less capable than himself. That strain, I believe, is what produced the characteristically ironic and sarcastic humour of which he is master. True, he told Lord Moran that his family life was so normal that he did not feel the pressure of his manifold public activities in the way another man might; and he has been exceptionally fortunate in his two marriages. But, from time to time there has been an indication that he felt the pressure of his self-ordained mode of existence.

I have quoted Harold Wilson's remark to the effect that his accession to the Mastership of Trinity made it possible for Butler to justify himself to his family's tradition. A combination of arrogance, humility and obstinacy was evident in him at a very early age. He sat an examination for Eton, which he failed. He had the temerity, however, to cross-examine the supervising master on whether or not a mistake had been made in failing him. The matter being resolved against him, the family, and particularly his mother, decided he should go to Harrow. The school was practically a colony of the Butler family: his grandfather had been Headmaster and at the time of this decision he had relations there both teaching and as pupils. He dug his heels in, particularly resistant, if I judge him correctly, to the idea of sharing a room with a cousin. Marlborough was chosen as an alternative, and even there the supposed advantages were that it was near an uncle's home and that it was the *alma mater* of a cousin (Charles Sorley, the poet) who had been killed in the First World War. The combination of elements in his reasoning, as in his wit, is instructive: he wanted Eton; he rejected Harrow because it was close to the family; and he accepted Marlborough which was not quite as close.

The arrogance has surfaced often since the Eton examination. It was the subject of a typically shrewd observation by Stanley Baldwin – of the seven Prime Ministers Butler served the one, he says himself, he most revered. Butler spoke in the debate on the 1930 Finance Bill. Afterwards Baldwin said to him, 'That was a good speech, Rab. But I got damn bored. You went too fast; you need not think everybody has a quick brain.' 'Baldwin', says Butler caustically, 'could certainly never be accused of going too fast.'

There is no doubt at all about the genuineness of Butler's admiration for Baldwin, and for the ameliorative Tory tradition Baldwin (and his uncle Geoffrey) represented. To Churchill Baldwin was the supreme party leader of his time. To Butler he was much more, a moral as well as a political force. Even so, Butler cannot resist putting Baldwin down. He tells of an occasion when Baldwin came to visit Saffron Walden. He praises lavishly Baldwin's ability immediately to enter into the spirit of his country audience, but observes that the then Prime Minister's apparent acquaintance with the current popular novelist – which delighted his hearers – had been obtained by 'fingering and sniffing' her works in Butler's own library. He tells, also, of a much earlier occasion, when he opposed Baldwin in a debate at the Cambridge Union. This was in 1924, when Baldwin was in opposition. Butler, as President, cast the deciding vote against the leader of his party. The following morning he, as host, took Baldwin to Cambridge railway station and 'he took me over to the bookstall and bought me a shocker, saying that the sin of intellectualism was worse than death'. He goes on to observe that Baldwin had suffered under his own great-uncle, Montagu, at Harrow, particularly because he had been found with an indecent book in his room.

As always,, it is exceptionally hard to tell where Butler wishes the permanent emphasis to be placed in such stories as these. He has a good deal of fun, throughout his memoirs, at Baldwin's expense. He has fun at the expense of Lord Halifax also, whose record as Viceroy of India and subsequently as Foreign Secretary, he says he admired just this side of idolatry. Nevertheless, he makes a joke of the fact that Baldwin's wife called him 'Tiger', that his allies called him 'Bonzo' and that his intimates referred to him as 'God'. 'This got us into trouble', Butler wrote, 'whenever Edward Halifax appeared, because he had ideas about who God really was.' Much of this might be taken as rather gentle humour; but it is observable that Butler almost never jokes, in print or in conversation, about or against his family. He writes in a touching way about both his wives, and especially about his son Adam, a minister in Mrs Margaret Thatcher's government. He is not blind to the faults of his father – a lack of humour and an insensitivity to Indian art among them – but he writes directly about them. He says himself that he is banal and almost ludicrously sentimental about his mother, his supreme love for whom he finds himself unable to express except in the baldest terms, and in nothing like the prose style he feels that love merits. No colleague or friend receives that kind of devotion and kindness at his hands. I therefore conclude that, for all his early resistance to some of the views of his family, all the multifarious members of it have had his loyalty; and that no political ally or friend has truly enjoyed it to any degree. Everybody in his professional life has at one time or another been a victim of his irony.

And yet there has been about him in practice a directness and warmth which is rare in senior politicians. I have mentioned the assiduity with which he nursed his constituency for a generation. I have emphasized his devotion to the people of India. It would be unimaginable for Butler to say of the Indians, as Churchill did in the great parliamentary debates of 1933:

> The 100 million new human beings are here to greet the dawn, toil upon the plains, bow before the temples of inexorable gods. They are here. You cannot desert them, you cannot abandon them. They are as much children as any children could be.

'This', says Butler, again caustically, 'was fine, colourful and brilliant stuff.' It failed to move him, not simply because it was so highly rhetorical, but because he found it patronizing; and he could not bear to have Indians patronized.

'Rab is behaving very well,' Churchill said of him once. 'The party has great confidence in him. He scorns to play for popularity, just does what he thinks is right.' This considerable testimony did not, however, extend to supporting Butler against Eden when Churchill himself retired. Nor would Churchill lend his support to Butler in 1957 when the Palace sought his advice on who should be asked to succeed Eden: Churchill was uncompromisingly for Macmillan. It is unlikely in the extreme that Churchill was influenced in his suspicion of Butler either by the fact that he had supported the pre-war appeasement policy or by their long parliamentary quarrels of the thirties in India. Indeed, in 1953, when Eden was eagerly and occasionally pushily anticipating a succession which had been practically assured to him, but which Churchill was continually and fretfully putting off, Butler was often on

Churchill's side. In July of that year, for example, Lord Moran tells us that Butler was one of the few in the inner circle of government who was hopeful of a physical and political comeback by Churchill. However, Churchill told Moran, 'Rab is very efficient up to a point, but he is narrow and doesn't see beyond his nose.' Harold Macmillan had a more spacious imagination and thus, when asked for his views in 1957, Churchill commended him. He was, it must be said, even more doubtful about Eden than he was about Butler; but by the time of his own retirement the expectation that Eden would follow him was too great for him to do more than grumble about it.

As Churchill was reserved about Butler so, even to this day, Butler is reserved about Churchill. He pays, in speech and in writing, the conventional tributes to the nation's saviour of 1940. He points out, however, that the coinage of alarm which Churchill used in his denunciations of Nazism had already been devalued by its excessive usage in his attacks on Baldwin's and Macdonald's Indian policy – and, he might have added, by Churchill's support of Edward VIII in the argument over abdication, something which Churchill himself admitted. The point is shrewd and well-taken but it expresses, I feel, not just a sensible political view but a more general sense of unease on Butler's part in dealing with a character so much larger than life as Churchill. In his memoirs he has far more to say on Churchill and India than on Churchill and the war and this, I believe, is because he is much more at ease in discussing the man in relation to a subject where their differences were concrete, assessable and specific than one which his imagination could scarcely encompass. The ruthless and even fervid energy with which Churchill had all his life pursued both the public good and high office was something Butler never possessed and, perhaps, could not even understand. When the last opportunity came his way in 1963 he would not, as we have seen, fight. On the previous occasion (in 1957) when Macmillan was his direct rival he was also deficient in the art of political combat. As Brendan Bracken wrote to Beaverbrook,

> Nor was Macmillan slow in his siege of No. 10. He let it be known that in no circumstances would he serve under Butler and he did powerful private canvassing. Of Butler, therefore, it may be truly said in the words of Coleridge – 'For I have lost the race I never ran.'

While throughout his life many of Butler's followers – Enoch Powell of their number expresses this view most forcefully – have been both hurt and disappointed by his lack of personal ambition and the lust for a fight it is by no means to his discredit. Indeed, I find his honest confession that he lacks the killer instinct in politics far preferable to Macmillan's conscious posturing: Bracken's devastating account of what Macmillan actually did in 1957 is far more convincing than Macmillan's own account of how the summons to the Palace to assume Eden's mantle found him sitting in No. 11 Downing Street (the residence of the Chancellor of the Exchequer) reading Jane Austen. Moreover, though Butler – scorning to play for popularity, just doing what he thought was right – was opposed to the Suez expedition from the beginning, Macmillan havered throughout and demonstrated single-mindedness not on matters of policy, but only in his pursuit of Eden's job, being, as Bracken wrote to W. S. Robinson, 'a very remarkable man, imaginative, amusing and possessed of a judgement which is almost always wrong'.

On entering the House of Commons, Butler did not forget there the concerns to which he had addressed himself in his constituency. In the short period before be became a minister, he dealt mainly with agricultural questions arising out of the preoccupations of Saffron Walden. He and his wife kept their promise to live in the constituency (for the first five years at Broxted, and subsequently at Stanstead Hall). He continued, apace, to deepen his identification with the area, and even served as a churchwarden for thirty-six years. His four children – Richard, a farmer, Adam, a government minister, James, a public relations specialist, and Sarah – were all brought up there and shared to the full their parents' involvement in local life.

However, given his connections, his ambitions and the political education with which he had sought to provide himself during his and Sydney's world tour, there was little likelihood that Butler would settle down to being a backbench agricultural specialist. Immediately upon his arrival at Westminster he joined a backbench group derisively known as 'the Boys' Brigade', the principal purpose of which (though its general character was what is called progressive) was to help the Tory Whips. Much further to the left than the Brigade was Harold Macmillan, then fighting an almost solitary battle against the government's domestic policy. It was this divergence of view, as will shortly be related, that led to the first clash between the two men. Meanwhile, in the early months of the new Parliament, Butler carefully and diligently cultivated his seniors in the party, and made himself greatly agreeable to them. The reputation for loyalty to the party line which he thus acquired did much to overcome what might otherwise have been thought of as his excessive intellectualism.

Of the very early part of his ministerial life – when he was first Parliamentary Private Secretary to the Secretary of State for India and subsequently the junior minister at the India office – Butler observes that he was saddened by the fact that John Simon, Samuel Hoare and even Edward Halifax all represented progressive government policy on India to the Conservative Party as the only way to discredit the rebellious youth of the subcontinent. '...I knew', he wrote, 'that what had failed to capture the young mind of India could not endure'. This judgement is symbolic of his whole political career. He called his memoirs *The Art of the*

Possible, and he stresses again and again in their course that his reasons throughout his life for being less radical and less outspoken than his admirers would have liked – on India, on education, on appeasement, on the leadership of the party – were essentially related to what was politically practicable at a given time. But the truth is more to his credit: once he had defined a trend, something he thought was right or, even, something he thought was inevitable, he pursued it with the utmost rigour, devotion, and probity. His successes and failures alike, the issues on which hindsight tells he was correct and also those on which he was wrong, all exemplify that strength of character of which it is very easy to lose sight because of his lack of ruthlessness for himself.

Butler remains immensely proud of his work at the India Office, and is particularly pleased by his own conviction that he got the better of Churchill, not simply in the course of their parliamentary exchanges, but in the equally crucial struggle for control of the Conservative machine in the country, in which Churchill and his right-wing allies were very nearly successful. The fight over India marked Butler down as being of the reformist wing of the party, and it is easy to see it as being all of a piece with his subsequent reputation as an enlightened Education Minister and a remarkably liberal (with the exception of the introduction of the first Immigration Act) Home Secretary. In fact, however, it was by no means as easy as that judgement implies to define his political coloration in the pre-war period.

The real genius of the Conservative left at that time was not Butler, but Harold Macmillan. Until very recently when the republication of his pre-war book *The Middle Way* helped to set the record straight on the domestic policies he favoured in his youth, Macmillan's subsequent passionate support for Churchill in the matter of policy towards Germany has often tended to obscure the extent to which he was in advance of his party on social and economic policy. Indeed, he sometimes went so far in this direction that Clement Attlee at one time believed that he might join the Labour Party and he did, for a time, sever his connection with the Tories.

What brought Macmillan back into the mainstream of the Conservative Party was the war, and specifically Churchill's appointment of him – with ministerial rank – to head the British mission to North Africa. Butler speaks, not without a certain bitterness, of the fact that, ultimately, Macmillan's rebellion against the party leadership in the 1930s was thus rewarded, for he himself had all this time been the quintessence of loyalty. It is a striking fact about his career not simply that it was so long, and spanned such a variety of jobs, but that for its entire duration (with the exception of his first few months in the House of Commons, when the National Government was in power) he held office whenever his party was in power, and sat on the front bench when it was not. Given the economic and social policies of the governments of the thirties, therefore, it was not open to the young Butler, determined not to be a rebel, to take his place in the van of so-called progressive political thinking; that had to await the post-war period and the Chairmanship of the Conservative Research Department.

But Macmillan and Butler knew one another well in those pre-war years and Macmillan seems, indeed, to have treated Butler as something of an unofficial Conservative Whip, through whom he could channel his increasingly bitter complaints about the party leadership. In recalling one of their conversations Butler underlines – I think unwittingly – the crucial difference between them in the matter of settling the relative importance of different areas of policy. Baldwin had declared to Butler his tactical ambition to steer a middle course between Macmillan and Sir Henry Page-Croft, one of the leaders of the die-hard right. Macmillan was fully aware of this and extremely resentful of the fact that, whereas the government relied on himself and his likeminded friends to beat off the attacks from the right on its Indian policy, it relied on Page-Croft and the right to beat off Macmillanite attacks on its social and economic policies. He therefore, according to Butler, threatened to forge an alliance with Page-Croft under the terms of which the left would allow the right a free hand on India in return for the right's steadfast support for a progressive economic and social, essentially Keynesian policy. Nor was such an alliance – though nothing ever came of it – inherently impossible, for there has always been a paternalist strain in the Tory right, and a willingness to balance a strong foreign and imperial policy with an ameliorative domestic one. Churchill, after all, who emerged during the Indian debates as the most substantial figure on the right wing, had been, with Lloyd George, the creator of unemployment insurance and Labour Exchanges; there was no time in his career when he did not look at least in a kindly way on schemes for social welfare, and he often supported such schemes with great enthusiasm, as Butler was to discover after 1945.

But there is no doubt that Butler was profoundly shocked by Macmillan's threat. There were two reasons for this. In the first place, like Baldwin, Butler thought the issue of India's movement towards independence, with Dominion status, was the issue of the day, compared to which nothing else was of the first importance. But the second reason cuts even more deeply into his nature: he was not loyal to his leadership for reasons of calculation or cowardice, but from the deepest motives of temperament and conviction. For all his intellectual arrogance, for all his cruel wit, for all his willingness verbally to wound – all traits which ultimately cost him the highest office – he could not make himself into a rebel. Of course, in the thirties there was not really much for him to rebel about, for he was convinced that the Macdonald, Baldwin and Chamberlain governments were correct in all three main areas of policy – economic, foreign and Indian. There is no doubt, however, that he did have a certain amount of sympathy with Macmillan's social ideas, but that did not allow him to countenance what he saw straightforwardly as disloyalty. Even in later years, when he opposed Eden's Suez policy root and branch, he never contemplated resignation, nor uttered more than mild protests. If they had studied his career and character with sufficient care, therefore, Macleod and Powell would have known how small was the chance in 1963 of persuading Butler to stage a *démarche* by refusing to serve under Home, and thus splitting the party, however temporarily.

Of course, political parties exist by and through such loyalty. No party could long survive – and certainly not enjoy the extraordinary success that attends the historical record of the Conservative Party – without possessing, both in Parliament and in the country, an army of foot-soldiers whose first political instinct is to obey. Neither of the other major British parties, moreover, has shown anything like the tenacity and skill of the Tories in creating and maintaining such loyalty. Loyalty, it was once said, is the Tory secret weapon, and even if Labour critics in particular frequently attack the Conservative Party for its ruthless treatment of fading leaders the fact remains that other parties envy the Tories the vast ranks of their submissive and industrious supporters in every part of the country.

What is unusual, however, at any rate in Parliament, is to find such reliability and steadfastness in a man of Butler's ability. Party Whips are skilled – and, again, Tory Whips are more skilled than most – both at soothing the egos and quieting the doubts of backbenchers. They are skilled, too, at exciting the cupidity of those who are loyal from calculation, though such men rarely receive the reward of office which they seek. But first-class ability, and a brain of Butler's calibre, usually leads, at some point in a career, to rebellion. Churchill, until old age, was one of nature's rebels, ever willing to be the only man in step, ever keen for the fray, ever happy to justify conduct which others – often even his own family – thought outrageous. He left the Tories for the Liberals and then, after flirting with independence, returned to the fold, observing that any fool could rat, but that it took a certain amount of genius to rat twice. It also took, of course, a good deal of brash and unquestioning self-confidence. In our own time Enoch Powell, though he is a very different kind of man from Churchill, represents the same proposition that ability and independence so often go hand in hand. Powell is by nature a loner, not at all, as he says himself, a good team man. During his time on the Conservative front bench after the 1964 election defeat he was a constant irritation to his colleagues because of his tendency to step out of line. After his dismissal by Edward Heath in 1968, and as long as he remained a member of the party, he took, it often seemed, a perverse delight in being in a minority of one on a whole host of issues, even when he did not command the national support he excited by his stand on the issue of immigration. Eden resigned on an issue of foreign policy, Macleod refused to serve under Home and, although resignation from a government on an issue of principle is far rarer nowadays than it once was, there are a number of front-rank politicians of both major parties whom one could see taking that course.

All this is foreign to Butler; it puzzles and saddens him. He once visibly shuddered when I quoted to him an aphorism of Powell's to the effect that the crucial test of a politician was how many resignations he had in him (though Powell himself has never resigned *office* except on the occasion when, with Peter Thorneycroft and Nigel Birch, he left the Treasury on the issue of Macmillan's public spending policy; he merely refused to serve Home and was dismissed by Heath, while his most spectacular *coup de théâtre* was his decision not to stand at all for Parliament in February 1974).

Of course, it is also fair to say of Butler, as he says himself, that despite the length of his political life he has simply never found himself very much at odds with the Conservative leadership of the day. The exception to that generalization, of course, is Suez. However, it is most improbable for a man of such developed intelligence never, over that extraordinary period, to have found himself in a state of incipient rebellion. Indeed, in addition to factors I have already discussed which, I believe, helped to form Macmillan's determination in 1963 that Butler should not succeed him, I believe there was also a profound suspicion that the unbroken and even tenor of his whole political life indicated very strongly that this was not a man of the toughness and often bloody-mindedness needed to pull a badly demoralized party together, run the country at a time of serious crisis and win a general election – all within a year.

Butler never achieved quite what he wanted for India. Although the Government of India Act finally passed through all its stages, though it set the pattern of parliamentary government in India, and though Nehru subsequently told Butler that it formed the basis of the post-war Independence Act itself, he was nevertheless discontented, and is still rather bitter about the opposition of both Churchill and his friends and of the Indian Princes to it, which opposition, he believes, led ultimately to the creation of Pakistan and the bloodshed which followed the Mountbatten settlement. For this reason, though he looks back with great affection and warmth to his days at the India Office, he does not compare his time there with his subsequent stint at the Department of Education.

He was also, as he admits, tired by 1936. As he points

out himself, the debates on the India Act ran to fifteen and a half million words, and he had taken part in most of them. Then Hoare, his chief, of whom he was very fond, was moved to the Foreign Office and Lord Zetland, who succeeded him, excited nothing like the same loyalty, being a man of singular arrogance and coldness of personality, observing once to Butler, who had asked him what steps he should take to improve his feel for poltical affairs, 'Read my books'. He was thus relieved to be offered a stint at the Ministry of Labour under Ernest Brown, and he marked time there until, in February 1938, he was offered the Parliamentary Under-Secretaryship at the Foreign Office under his old friend Lord Halifax, the former Viceroy. He was, however, quite scathing about the post, observing that he read the Labour department's standing orders only in the lavatory, whither he carried them in his hip pocket.

But Butler had hankered after the Foreign Office. Indeed, he was subsequently, in 1957, to ask Macmillan to make him Foreign Secretary. The request was denied and it was not until 1963, when Home gave him a completely open choice of office, that he finally realized his ambition. In spite of that long-held wish, however, and in spite of the fact that he has tremendous skills as a diplomat and, particularly, as a negotiator, I do not think foreign affairs is Butler's long suit. In domesic affairs he has always shown great finesse at defining issues and selecting between paths. During both his stints at the Foreign Office (though even taken together they were of such short duration that a really hard and fast judgement is difficult to make) he seemed to sink into the atmosphere of the place and the business of international diplomacy all too readily. But, of course, one says that in the full consciousness of the fact that, if not one of its architects, he was and remains one of the most eloquent defenders of the policy of appeasement.

3
Appeasement

Of course Butler could not, in 1938, and cannot now, be blamed in any way for the slowness of the Baldwin and Chamberlain governments to realize the nature of the threat emanating from Nazi Germany. His chapter in his memoirs on foreign policy from early 1938 to the outbreak of war is, however, one of the most crucial in his book. It appeared in 1971, at a significant time when revisionist historians were already beginning to question what appeared to them to be the excessively simplistic attack mounted on appeasement, first and principally in Churchill's history of the war, but also in such works as Sir John Wheeler-Bennett's *Munich: Prologue to Tragedy*. Butler's thesis is straightforward and robustly expressed. There are none of the lighter touches which grace so much of the rest of the book and he makes no bones about where he stands.

However, the exact and to some degree limited nature of his argument has to be appreciated, as have certain qualifications, reservations and excuses which are embedded in

Chamberlain and his Foreign Secretary, Halifax, Butler's friend and chief. Butler does not seek to defend the whole foreign policy of the thirties. He confines himself, in essence, to a defence of the Munich agreement by which Czechoslovakia was dismembered, and which called forth from Churchill probably his finest pre-war speech on foreign policy in the House of Commons. To Butler, Munich was a necessity, a regrettable and distasteful necessity, perhaps, but one that gained crucial time in which to speed up British rearmament and seek to recreate a system of collective security. Although he insists that Britain was much stronger in September 1939 than she was at Munich, he goes on frankly to admit the possibility of arguing convincingly that the situation over Poland was not all that much different from the situation over Czechoslovakia. He also implies, without stating it directly, that the decision to offer a guarantee of Poland's territorial integrity – which Chamberlain put forward immediately after Germany had swallowed up what had been left of Czechoslovakia after what amounts to a forensically skilful essay in defence of Munich – was a quixotic one.

There are certain other aspects of his argument and certain lacunae in it which, while not as crucial as the elements in his case outlined above, are nevertheless important not merely for their substance but also because they represent the Butler style, in some ways at its most characteristic. First, Butler, while offering his defence, exculpates himself from all blame, observing that, as a junior minister he bore little responsibility and was rarely consulted. Secondly, he defends Halifax with rare warmth and passion, insisting that from the moment of the Polish guarantee Halifax turned his back on the whole doctrine of appeasement and set his face resolutely against Germany. Thirdly, he insists that, if not as firm as early as Halifax, Chamberlain himself shared his Foreign Secretary's resolution when the crunch came; and Butler goes out of his way to praise, for its style as well as its content, a bellicose speech made by Chamberlain on 17 March 1939. Fourthly and finally, he denies that the Chamberlain government had any policy of excluding Russia from Western Europe (a favourite criticism of Churchill's), and insists, rather, that the Russians simply refused to involve themselves. None of these points is wholly true.

Let us take, first, Butler's own responsibility and attitudes. It is certainly the case, as he argues, that he had no responsibility for formulating the policy against which Churchill was launching his Phillipics. That policy, and even its development into something else after the guarantee to Poland, was already set in amber before he came to the Foreign Office in February 1938. But Butler did not merely go along with appeasement: he worked hard, long and enthusiastically for it, and there is very little evidence in the public records for the time that he took the slightest contemporary interest in the rearmament programme to which he devotes such emphasis in his memoirs. He is inconsistent in his account of the degree to which he enjoyed real responsibility. While at one point he denies such responsibility, at another he points out that he and Halifax shared almost equally the anxious and (if German) minatory foreign guests they had to see in the course of diplomatic business. Moreover, the Foreign Office of 1938 and 1939 was not the Foreign Office of today: there were only two ministers, and Halifax was in the House of Lords, so a great part of the burden of defining and defending the government's policy in the crucial chamber fell to Butler. It is true, of course, that Neville Chamberlain was the real architect of his own government's foreign policy, and it was his combination of jealous secretiveness and domineering interference in the conduct of that policy that had led to Anthony Eden's resignation. Still, Butler had a lot to do, and the bulk of what he said on foreign affairs for public consumption was out and out supportive of his chiefs, with only the the most generalized and conventional references to the necessity of building up Britain's military strength.

It is about this time – from his arrival at the Foreign Office – that we can begin to see that taste for ambiguity and even deviousness which has done Butler so much harm throughout his career. It was about this time that he began to be all things to all men. He chose as his Parliamentary Private Secretary Henry 'Chips' Channon, a choice which, since Channon was one of the most enthusiastic of all appeasers, hardly suggests that Butler found any of the policy disagreeable or distasteful. Channon was devoted to Neville Chamberlain and his diaries are full of fulsome appreciation of Butler's similar devotion and stout loyalty.

On the other hand, and in the opinion of most scholars far more reliable and perceptive, we have the diaries of Harold Nicolson. Nicolson was an implacable critic of appeasement, and close to Eden and Churchill. He was a writer and analyst of real distinction; he had been a diplomat; and he was the son of Lord Carnock, a great Ambassador and Permanent Under-Secretary at the Foreign Office. Butler puzzled Nicolson: in public he seemed loyal to Chamberlain and Halifax, but in private there were many shades to his conversation. Nicolson's entry for 12 October 1939 reads:

> Walk away from the Foreign Office with Rab Butler. He asks me what I would like the Prime Minister to say this afternoon in reply to Hitler's peace offer. I said I should like a speech saying quite shortly that we are only too anxious to make peace but that we must have a guarantee before entering a conference. That guarantee would be the withdrawal of German troops from Prague and Warsaw. He laughs and says, 'I am afraid that that sounds rather like appeasement. The Prime Minister is much more bellicose than that.' He is a curious man. I

> have a suspicion that he does not really agree with the appeasement policy and has all along been on our side. He has seen in some paper that I was writing this Penguin Special and he asked me if he could see the proofs. I said, 'There is a great deal in the book which will annoy the Government terribly.' He answered, 'It won't annoy me!'

The Penguin Special was called *Why Britain Is at War*. Nicolson discussed it during a long talk with Butler the following December:

> He tells me my book is a work of art and perfectly correct. He thinks that I am right about Chamberlain and Horace Wilson [Chamberlain's closest adviser; Nicolson was intensely hostile to them both] in so far as diplomacy is concerned, but that Horace is really a very gifted man nonetheless. He says that his influence over Chamberlain is something extraordinary and that the latter simply cannot move without him. He says that Chamberlain is tough without being strong.

The general implication of Nicolson's view of Butler based on these and other conversations was that he had all along been uneasy about appeasement, but had never been powerful enough to assert his doubts against the resolution of the Prime Minister, Wilson, and Halifax. But, as I have already argued, Butler was in fact a highly enthusiastic advocate of the policy. It is not possible here to go into all the strange ins and outs of the feeble, groping fashion in which British foreign policy was conducted between Munich and the outbreak of war, but there is some highly significant evidence about Butler's attitude in June 1939.

In June, Halifax – by now, according to Butler and his memoirs, settled on a strong policy against Germany – decided, in the words of Sidney Aster in *The Making of the Second World War*, 'to test the mood in Berlin'. He was influenced to some extent in this decision by Henderson, the British Ambassador in Berlin, and an arch appeaser. On 8 June Halifax addressed the House of Lords. He complained about the German occupation of Czechoslovakia, but the heart of his speech was – and despite predictably critical references to it in German newspapers was understood in Germany to be – concilatory, for any of Germany's further claims in Europe 'are', he said, 'open to consideration round a table'. Even that, however, was not enough for Butler. Already, the previous April, after a conversation with the pro-German Duke of Buccleuch, Butler had sent a minute to Halifax. He wrote: 'We have had a certain success in our "offensive diplomacy", that is, in active diplomacy, and now there is great room for healing diplomacy to follow.' The essence of Butler's argument was that talks should be encouraged between Germany and Poland, with a view to concessions by Poland over Danzig, and between Italy and France over their mutual problems in the Mediterranean. 'A dual system of offensive and healing diplomacy may well relieve tension without sacrificing our vital interests.' Now, on 13 June, Butler wrote again to Halifax enthusiastically advocating unilateral appeasement. The time was ripe, he thought, for reopening discussions with Germany with a view to placating her through concessions on trade, raw materials and colonies. These papers are not those of a man with any doubts about his policy.*

If Butler was prodding Halifax in the middle of the year, there was no need to prod either the Foreign Secretary or the Prime Minister in the days following the German attack on Poland; indeed, the conduct of Chamberlain and Halifax in the brief period between the attack and the British declaration of war, demonstrating as it did both

* These letters are to be found in the Public Record Office FO 800/315, H/XV/177.

the spinelessness and deceit of the House of Commons, completely explodes Butler's arguments about the new firmness of his two chiefs. The so-called Premier files (essentially, the files of Horace Wilson, kept at No. 10 Downing Street) and Cabinet and Foreign Office records available in the Public Record Office show that appeasement was still very much alive until the righteous fury of the House of Commons forced Chamberlain into a declaration.*

Germany attacked Poland at dawn on 1 September 1939. Early in the morning Churchill left Chartwell for London and Halifax assured the Polish Ambasador that Britain would stand by her guarantee. At an 11.30 a.m. Cabinet meeting the position seemed to be clear that no talks with Germany were possible while Poland was being violated. Halifax told his colleagues that he had already stated that explicitly to Ciano, the Italian Foreign Minister. But the Cabinet decided not to send an ultimatum to Germany but, rather, a warning.

In the course of the afternoon Chamberlain saw Churchill and offered him a post in the War Cabinet which he accepted. His acceptance had for Chamberlain the singular advantage of muzzling Churchill during the subsequent exchanges in the House of Commons. At six o'clock that evening Chamberlain addressed a tense, angry and crowded House. Under questioning he misled the House about the instructions that had been sent to Henderson in Berlin telling members that the Ambassador's instructions were to ask for his passports in the event of Germany refusing to withdraw from Poland. In the event, and even with the aid of this deception, Chamberlain's performance was ineffective and the House rose in a mood of great unease.

---

* This is not the place fully to analyse those strange days, but the interested reader will find a full account in the second chapter of my *Churchill at War* vol. I (1974).

That night Churchill wrote a comradely letter to Chamberlain. Not only did he receive no reply, but he had no communication at all from the Prime Minister during the whole of the following day. 'I thought it probable', Churchill later wrote, 'that a last-minute effort was being made to preserve peace; and this proved true.'

What happened was this. The House was due to meet at 2.45 p.m. on 2 September, to hear a statement from the Chancellor, Sir John Simon, on emergency financial matters. At 2.30 p.m. Ciano telephoned Halifax offering Italian mediation between Britain and Germany. Halifax immediately rushed over to the House of Commons to postpone Simon's statement. He then got in touch with Ciano, and with Henderson, whom he instructed to tell Ribbentrop, the German Foreign Minister, that earlier communications from Britain were definitely not ultimata. Britain was supposed to insist, and the Italians declined to insist, that a German withdrawal from Poland should precede an armistice and a conference; but Halifax did not press this too hard, offering, instead, to consult Chamberlain.

Meanwhile Alexander Cadogan spoke to Bonnet, the French Foreign Minister, who clearly did not think that German retirement from Poland should be a pre-condition for an armistice. The Cabinet then met, at 4.15 p.m. Halifax had already consulted Chamberlain, and told him of Bonnet's view that there should be a delay of forty-eight hours to enable Hitler to reconsider. He and the Prime Minister, however, found the Cabinet in an extremely tough mood and were forced against their wills (which is evident from the minutes) to agree that no negotiation should be attempted until the German army had left Poland, and that Hitler should be given no later than until midnight to make his reply.

The House of Commons had been told that Chamberlain would speak at six o'clock in the evening. Then the speech was postponed, to allow further consultations with Ciano. By now the mood of members was turning ugly and Churchill was in a state of growling resentment. At 7.45 p.m. Chamberlain arrived. He told them what had been going on, but he offered no policy. 'Members', wrote General Edward Spears in his diary, 'sat as if turned to stone. The shock was such that for a moment there was no more movement than there was sound when the Prime Minister sat down.' 'It was evident', commented Nicolson, 'when he sat down that no decision had been arrived at.' There followed the famous speech by the Labour deputy leader Arthur Greenwood, which was preceded by Robert Boothby's cry, '*You* speak for England.'

Halifax and Chamberlain were both badly shaken. They dined together at No. 10 and a Cabinet was summoned for 11.30 that evening. It was obvious that the appeasement position could not be held, particularly when Chamberlain heard that the other members of the Cabinet had met at the House and resolved to force their two leaders into a declaration of war. Chamberlain gave way and at 11.15 the following morning broadcast an announcement that war had begun. At no stage, therefore, was his conduct, or that of Halifax, remotely as Butler describes it: they havered and wavered and dithered to the very last.

Even with all the evidence we now have available it is difficult in the extreme to enter fully into the spirit of the reasoning of Halifax and Chamberlain at this time or, for that matter, the reasoning of Butler. Even his account of British policy towards Russia – based on the proposition that it was impossible to conclude an alliance with the Soviet Union because the Russians would not co-operate – does not bear much examination. It may be that such an alliance was impossible to conclude. It was certainly true that even had she been willing to help Czechoslovakia the USSR would have found it impossible to obtain permission to march her troops through Poland or Rumania. But it is wrong to suggest or imply that Chamberlain and Halifax tried. Butler, it is true, saw a good deal of the Russians, and especially of Litvinov. But Halifax always refused to see Russian ministers or diplomats if he could possibly avoid it, and Chamberlain returned stony answers to American pleas that an effort should be made to achieve common cause with Stalin. It may be (and I tend to think so) that no effort would have made much difference to Stalin's policy; but it is disingenuous to imply that the British government was willing.

In a remarkably interesting essay published in 1961 in the *Transactions of the Royal Historical Society* John Ehrman compared Churchill and Lloyd George as war ministers. He quoted F.S. Oliver on the peculiarly demonic power Lloyd George brought to the management of the war machine, and how his deadly, bustling, driving personality contrasted with the increasingly feeble vacillations of Asquith. Ehrman argues that Churchill possessed a like force, and that the simple fact of the matter was that the leaders of the Chamberlain government did not. Churchill himself realized that there was something about himself that made him different from other men in war. It occasionally worried him, and he wrote to his wife at the beginning of the First World War expressing his exhilaration now that the hour had come and accusing himself for the way he felt. This inherent element of character gave him, as it had given Lloyd George, a special ability in war. It was not that Churchill did not make mistakes, often important ones. But his restless, disciplined energy, the sheer deadliness (as his wife once called it) of his personality gave him the strength to pull the whole wartime government together, and to go over to the offensive almost immediately. It was his possession of that spirit rather than the fact that he had foretold the war that made him indispensable in 1940.

Chamberlain, Halifax and Butler were all intrinsically

men of peace. By that I do not mean that they were cowards, or that they refused to contemplate war. It is true that there was throughout British society in the thirties a shrinking from the very idea that it might be necessary to fight again, because of memories of the carnage wreaked between 1914 and 1918. But what I am trying to describe is an inner and almost spiritual reluctance to contemplate international conflict and, by extension, an imaginative inability to grasp that Hitler would go on until he was stopped: he would push at every door he found open. Indeed, up to the very last moment in September 1939 he was convinced Britain and France would not fight and that, if they did, they would be brushed aside. His conviction of the decadence of the Western democracics was, indeed, an important part of what drove Hitler so steadily towards war.

Men like Chamberlain and Halifax and Butler were simply not made to understand such a character. We have seen that in June Butler was still convinced that a bargain could be struck with Hitler and Germany. And that conviction did not come – none of the available papers suggests that it did – from a belief that it was necessary to wait until Britain was strong again before meeting the German challenge. It sprang from the faith that international politics, like all politics, was the art of the possible, that the political world was a world in which deals were made – it existed for the making of deals – and that therefore, while pursuing in a leisurely way the requirements of constructing a system for collective security, the really important thing was to find the key to Germany's ambitions, to find the terms on which Hitler would finally settle. It is true that Chamberlain at last gave the guarantee to Poland. It is true that, after the final conquest of Czechoslovakia, he swore in private that he would never trust Hitler again. But, as we have seen, as late as 2 September he was still seeking a way out, at a time when the slightest delay (as the defence chiefs argued) was dangerous to the armed forces, and could have been extremely dangerous to public morale.

It was, of course, ironic that Chamberlain fell in May 1940 and was replaced by Churchill as a result of the failure of a campaign (in Norway) which Churchill had himself instigated and prosecuted. But Churchill's errors of judgement and the reverses he suffered were far less than the sum of his qualities, his personal magnetism, his oratory, his fighting spirit. None of the appeasers, and there were competent men among them, possessed remotely similar characteristics. Chamberlain, of course, though he remained for a time in the Churchill government, became ill and shortly afterwards died. Churchill neither liked nor trusted Halifax – not least because as late as the fall of France he again raised in Cabinet the spectre of an approach to Mussolini to use his good offices to seek a negotiated settlement with Hitler – and shortly packed him off to the United States as Ambassador, replacing him at the Foreign Office by Eden, a man, despite his weaknesses, much more to his own taste. Finally, as we shall see in the next chapter, Butler was only too willing to leave the Foreign Office for the more tranquil pastures of the Department of Education, though, in the event, while the war was at its height, he could not gain Churchill's support for the reforms he wished to introduce.

It remains to be discussed whether, however inaccurate Butler's account of politics and diplomacy in the last months of peace is, there is not something to be said for his view that Munich was a necessity; that, in fact, Britain and France could not have fought for Czechoslovakia, and were better advised to bide their time and keep their powder dry.

There is, at present, much controversy over the scope and speed of British rearmament. It is certainly true, as Butler says, that the Royal Air Force was considerably stronger a year after Munich than it was at the time of the agreement. Although progress could have been quicker, it is also true to say that not as much time was wasted as Churchill alleged in his *History*. Nevertheless, Britain in 1939 *was* woefully ill-prepared for war, though it was in better shape than was thought at the time because Germany's strength, particularly in the air, had been overrated. On the other hand, German forces also increased enormously over that short period, and German rearmament was proceeding, and had been proceeding for years, at a far more furious pace than that of Britain. As Churchill has powerfully argued, every year that went by put Hitler in a stronger position, and made it harder for Britain to catch up. In many ways the Allies were fortunate that Hitler, against the advice of his generals, decided to start the war in 1939, rather than wait another couple of years at least.

There is another extremely important point: throughout the relevant chapter in his memoirs Butler argues that the Munich agreement was consciously made out of a realization of Britain's weakness and an awareness that time was needed to strengthen her defences; and this is not true. Butler does not say (as some writers more plausibly have said) that hindsight tells us that Munich was a gain; he insists that it was an act of foresight, and that that act of foresight was in part based on a correct appreciation of the strength of the German bomber force. It was vital, thus, to build up Fighter Command before the confrontation.

But the finest intelligence in British military and political circles at the time would not have expected a German attack on France (in 1938) to succeed, just as the most capable analysts did not, in 1939 or early 1940, expect anything like the consequences of the Battle of France. Poland was a different matter; but Poland was judged to be a third-class while France was a first-class power. In the event it took Germany only nine days longer to destroy France than Poland – thirty-six as against twenty-seven.

Now, once we appreciate that in 1938 it was assumed that the Maginot Line would hold (trench warfare was anticipated), than it was clear that German bombers would not have the range to reach Britain. It is absurd therefore to argue that strategic appreciation *at the time* influenced political decisions because of fear of the bomber. Until Germany took France and the Low Countries Britain could not be seriously assailed from the air.

Moreover, the Munich agreement meant the loss of Czechoslovakia. Butler argues that Chamberlain was much influenced in his approach to Hitler at the time of Munich by a military briefing which maintained that, after the German takeover of Austria, Czechoslovakia's lengthy border was indefensible. The Czech General Staff did not think so, and Czechoslovakia had one of the most efficient, respected and even admired armies in Europe. It was, moreover, a modern affair, unlike the gallant but wretchedly equipped Polish Army destroyed by the *Wehrmacht* in the first years of the war, and in morale and courage not at all like the French army which crumpled before the German advance in 1940.

The loss of the Czech Army was a severe blow to the Allies. Perhaps even more important, however, was the fact that by her occupation of Czechoslovakia, Germany gained possession of the giant Skoda iron and steel works, the finest of its kind in Europe, which was immediately placed on a war production footing. This was a tremendous accession of strength to the German arms industry and one over which Hitler never ceased to gloat.

Butler has a stronger point when he argues about the weakness of the RAF. There was a terrible fear in Britain, stemming from a remark made years previously by Stanley Baldwin that 'The bomber will always get through.' And there was no doubt that the RAF was weak, not least because of the Air Staff's insistence over the years on a programme of bomber construction at the expense of fighters. But I doubt if the improvement after Munich was more than accidentally strategic. As the minutes of the Military Coordination Committee for the first year of the war show, the British defence effort was haphazard, sluggish, inefficient and downright wasteful. It was, indeed, one of Churchill's principal contributions to the war effort as a member of the Military Coordination Committee to bring order and discipline into war production; and it was because of his experience of that Committee from September 1939 to May 1940 that on becoming Prime Minister he also made himself Minister for Defence, so that he could preside over its deliberations.

Roosevelt once asked Churchill to think of a title, a soubriquet, for the war of 1939–45. He tells us that he replied promptly, 'The unnecessary war'. He was right. There were several occasions during the early years of Hitler's rise when a determined Anglo-French alliance could have stopped him in his tracks without effort and with little blood. But Hitler had energy and determination and the Allies were exhausted and almost indifferent, while the United States had withdrawn from the world to contemplate her own affairs. There was also a feeling, in the twenties and thirties, that Germany had been badly treated at Versailles; Butler several times gives expression to this view. It can most effectively be symbolized by the opinion in Britain at the time of the German re-occupation of the Rhineland. At that time France wanted to act, but would not do so without Britain, and Britain would not act at any price. So Hitler went on.

Hitler was not a man that the appeasers could even begin to understand. It is certain that men like Chamberlain and Halifax did not share to any great degree the admiration for his revived Germany which, in the early years of his power at least, was widespread in British society. They even, it seems, thought the little man rather an embarrassing figure, with his strutting and his odd uniforms. But they never penetrated to the core of his savage mind and even more savage heart. He was to them a rather different kind of politician, granted, but he was a politician all the same. His country had come off badly from the First World War and from Versailles, and he was doing the best he could to restore her fortunes and reverse the deal. The inner evil of the man and the engine of death and destruction which he had created they did not even begin to grasp until it was far, far too late.

It was not so with Churchill. From very early on he saw with uncanny clarity the intimate interconnection between the domestic nature of Nazism and its aggressive foreign intentions. Not all those who stood out against appeasement and for rearmament shared his point of view: some were distressed by the roughness of the language Churchill used about Hitler personally and about the Nazi Party. Such men were more in the classical tradition of British foreign policy: they feared Germany not because of the intentions of her government, but because of her power. They wanted to rearm so that Britain could negotiate from strength, so that, ultimately, a deal could be forced from Hitler.

It was Churchill, again, who grasped the essential fact that Hitler had to be eliminated if there was to be peace in Europe. Even if baulked he would come back elsewhere, such was his evil genius. For these reasons Churchill argued for resistance at every stage, and particularly in the early stages. Even though revisionist history, both in Britain and in Germany, is beginning to suggest that a deal could have been done with Hitler, I feel quite sure that Churchill was right: the snake had to be scotched, sooner or later.

For all his intelligence Butler did not see this. He was too immersed in the business of government, in the orderly transactions of business, in the principles of peaceful co-existence, fully to apply his mind to the problem in the way Churchill, untrammelled by office, prophetic of vision and zealously combative of nature, could. There is little doubt that Butler showed considerable self-knowledge, and knowledge, particularly, of his own limitations, when he accepted the Prime Minister's offer of the Ministry of Education.

Perhaps the favourite short argument about why Butler did not become Prime Minister either in 1957 or in 1963 is that he was an appeaser. He scarcely ever adverts to that accusation himself though he knows perfectly well, of course, that it has often been made. As I have already observed, however, I do not believe that judgement to be wholly true, though I do think that the chapter in defence of appeasement up to a point in *The Art of the Possible* is a characteristically indirect reply to it. Certainly, Butler's role in the formulation and execution of the appeasement policy could not have been the sole reason why Macmillan dished him in 1963. Macmillan had, after all, originally wanted Lord Hailsham (Quintin Hogg) to succeed him and Hogg had certainly been a far more outspoken, and publicly known appeaser than Butler, particularly when he stood as the official Conservative candidate in the 1938 Oxford by-election (where his anti-appeasement Conservative opponent, interestingly, was backed strongly by a politically enthusiastic young undergraduate named Edward Heath). In so far as the memory of his role before the war, while he served in the Foreign Office, helped to militate against his ambitions in 1957 and 1963 – and I believe that to some extent it did – it was rather more because of the recollected duplicity of the appeasement policy than because of its spinelessness. To convey the essential argument here it is necessary again to go over some of the material already covered, and to discuss occasions on which Butler was falsely accused as well as occasions on which his enemies were in the right.

The point has already been made that Butler's wounding if opaque wit has, during his career, made him many enemies, especially among his targets. Distrust was also aroused, of course, by his habit of saying different things to different people even if – again characteristically – he made most of his observations at least a touch ambiguous. But there has also been a far deeper, and far more serious, accusation made against him that he is by nature not merely ambiguous and sharp-tongued but, even on very serious matters, duplicitous.

In the appeasement chapter of his own memoirs Butler points out that he was only a junior minister, and therefore not really responsible for the grand strategy of appeasement, even though he defends, in particular, the post-Munich period. He also points out, which is perfectly true, that the real architect of the policy – and of all British foreign policy of the time – was Chamberlain, victim of a syndrome that almost always (Baldwin was an exception) afflicts Prime Ministers who rise to power principally on their domestic records, of falling in love with the glamour and the intricacy of diplomacy. He implies that this statement distances him somewhat from the Prime Minister and, indeed, in so far as his account refers to personalities, it should be said that his enthusiasm for and devotion to Halifax was far stronger than to the Prime Minister. But Butler was socially at least far closer to Chamberlain than he suggests, not least because they shared a friendship with Chips Channon, and frequently met at his house (where, later, the Butlers stayed after their own home suffered bomb damage). And it is a striking fact that after the Cabinet meeting which took the final decision to go to war it was Butler who was chosen by Chamberlain to remain alone with him and to comfort him.

There was also an earlier and exceptionally closely guarded operation undertaken by Butler and Chamberlain together. This was on the vexed question, already mentioned, of the official British attitude to the possibility of an Anglo- or perhaps Western-Soviet alliance. While there was a certain amount of fringe opinion in Britain to the effect that this country should join with Germany in an alliance against Soviet Russia it is also the case that – particularly after Munich, and especially in the middle of 1939 – the dominant idea was that Britain should seek an alliance with the USSR. Increasing rumours of a Soviet-German pact, such as ultimately came about, greatly increased this pressure, which was fed both by the Americans and by Churchill. While it is perfectly true (as Butler says) that the probability was always that Stalin would turn down the idea of an agreement with Britain (not least because he had a shrewd idea of Chamberlain's real views) it is untrue to say that Britain tried really hard.

It is not necessary to go into the full detail of Anglo-Soviet negotiations in 1939, since our principal purpose is to describe what Butler did. According to Halifax, on 23 May Chamberlain reluctantly concluded that an attempt must be made. That day Sir Alexander Cadogan, the Permanent Under-Secretary at the Foreign Office, noted in his diary: 'P.M. apparently resigned to idea of Soviet alliance, but depressed.' Chamberlain now began to prepare a brief which while it apparently met the growing desire to make friends – or at least allies – of the Russians would be less than whole-hearted. And his principal assistant in its preparation was R.A. Butler.

Chamberlain's views on the USSR were no secret. 'I regard Russia as a very unreliable friend', he wrote to his sister on 9 April, '... with an enormous irritative power on others.' He feared that an alliance with Russia would drive Spain into the arms of the Axis and added that the Russians 'have no understanding of other countries' mentality or conditions & no manners, & they are working hand in hand with our Opposition'. By 20 May, according to Cadogan's diary, 'P.M. says he will resign rather than sign alliance with Soviet.' Of course, it is also true that Chamberlain had a powerful ideological opposition to Russia; but in his simple dislike of the country and its people he echoed his similar dislike of the United States and its people.

However, at the Cabinet meeting of 24 May the Prime Minister finally gave in, following Halifax's opening statement to the effect that if the West did not try, the Germans might well succeed. It was a view widely shared. It was not true, of course, that those in the Conservative Party who favoured an alliance with Russia – like Churchill – in any way sympathized with Stalin; rather, they sought a counterbalance to Nazi Germany. Not for the first time all the petulance and rather hysterical emotion were on Chamberlain's side.

The Cabinet minutes record Chamberlain's observation that 'The question of presentation, however, was of the utmost importance and his ... difficulties would be greatly decreased if ... the arrangements could be presented as an interpretation of the principles of the Covenant [of the League of Nations].' It is certain that Chamberlain thought that no alliance with Russia was possible or desirable, that he was determined that, if he was forced to make an offer, it would be couched in such terms as to constitute a personal triumph for himself, and that it would be of a character to prevent all real intimacy between the two countries. He wrote to his sister on 25 May and told her that he was pleased with the turn of events, particularly that he had got nearly all his own way in spite of the fact that he had only two supporters, the faithful Horace Wilson – and R.A. Butler. Together they concocted a scheme which

> gives the Russians what they want, but in form & presentation it avoids the idea of an Alliance & substitutes a declaration of *intentions* in certain circumstances in fulfilment of our obligation under Article XVI of the Covenant. It is really a most ingenious idea for it is calculated to catch all the mugwumps & at the same

> time by tying the thing up to Article XVI we give it a *temporary* [my italics] character.

The Russians declined the offer, as it was most likely they would do. But Butler cannot pretend that he or his Prime Minister tried as hard as they might.

A much more puzzling episode involving Butler, in which he was completely innocent, but from which certain suspicions about his character were made to arise relates to a conversation he had after the fall of France in 1940 with the Swedish Minister in London, Bjorn Prytz. At that time, of course, Hitler had begun to hope that, with France out of the war, Britain would come to agreement, and he could, eventually, turn his arms on Russia. On the basis of Prytz's report the Swedish Foreign Minister put it about that Butler represented an appeasing wing in the British government which was willing to contemplate, if not capitulation, then at least a deal with Germany. Prytz subsequently denied that any such construction could properly have been placed on his report, but word of the matter reached Churchill, who wrote to Halifax accusing Butler of defeatism. This was not inherently improbable considering that at about this time Halifax, Butler's boss, friend and hero had sought a Cabinet discussion on possible peace moves – something which again undermines Butler's portrayal of Halifax as resolute from 1939 onwards. Under the threat of the Prime Minister's anger, Butler prepared a full note of the conversation, and was cross-examined at length by Halifax, who wrote to Churchill on 27 June stoutly defending his Under-Secretary and concluding, 'I should be very sorry if you felt any doubt either about Butler's discretion or his complete loyalty to Government policy, of both of which I am completely satisfied.'

The matter was thus closed. The difficulty about episodes like this, of course, is that a man who uses ambiguity of language to such an extent as Butler does invariably leaves a trail of suspicion behind him. There is no evidence that Churchill was other than wholly convinced by Halifax's defence; and he soon promoted Butler. He found Butler a most loyal and supportive colleague in the 1951 government and, though he backed Macmillan in 1957 there is, again, no evidence that he had any great objections to Butler.

But as he advanced in seniority Butler accumulated many more such misunderstandings, on a wide variety of topics, and it became impossible for some of his colleagues to be quite sure of where he stood on specific issues. There was no doubting his general liberalizing approach to politics and government, but the details often became fuzzy, misunderstood or inaccessible to understanding because of their ambiguity. As Butler grew older I believe this ambiguity became a habit with him so that, seasoned as it was by his wit, it became all but impossible for any but his intimates to be quite sure where he stood, or what he was saying, at any given time. And not all of this evasion was pre-considered.

But I do believe that the pre-war chapter in his memoirs is a most thoughtful and well-crafted piece of work, subtly and strongly written, cunningly arranged, and demonstrating great power of mind and style. The only trouble with it is that it is wrong, incomplete where completeness is required, replete with documentation on such a trivial matter as *l'affaire* Prytz, quite unsupported by evidence on much more important matters such as the development of the foreign policy attitudes of Chamberlain and Halifax, and vague beyond reasonable historical requirement on Butler's own role in, and attitude to, affairs. It is often the case that the reception the argument of a writer gets – and especially a politician writing his autobiography – is coloured by the reviewers' and reading public's attitude to the man himself and to the place in intellectual esteem which his ideas enjoy at the time he publishes. Thus it was that, because of the attitudes of the revisionist historians mentioned at the beginning of this chapter, and because many reviewers, even if they were not out-and-out Butler-ites, thought Butler had been badly treated in 1963 and perhaps in 1957, that an ultimately shoddy piece of work such as the appeasement chapter was so respectfully received. And it was, of course, set in the centre of a book that is, in general, a very fine one. Thus it was hard to attack a part while praising the whole.

4
The Board of Education

It was evident to many, not least to his Parliamentary Private Secretary, Lord Dunglass (subsequently the Earl of Home and Prime Minister) that from the beginning of the war Chamberlain's grasp of power was slipping. Churchill was the driving force at the Military Coordination Committee and, if he often irritated his colleagues with his impetuosity, his insistence on having his own way, and his interminable speeches in committee, then there was goodly compensation for him in the steadily growing public esteem which he enjoyed.

It was widely felt, too, that there should be a National Government. But here there was an immediate snag: the Labour Party would not serve under Chamberlain, not at any price. As Butler recalls from conversations he had with Hugh Dalton and Herbert Morrison (and as is confirmed by the Attlee papers in Churchill College) Labour's preference was for Halifax as Prime Minister. This was a consummation devoutly to be wished by Butler. Halifax was his friend, and even his hero; he had served him loyally and with enjoyment at the Foreign Office and worked earlier with him on the Government of India Act. Also, Butler had certain fears for his own future if Churchill became Prime Minister: he had been closely associated with the appeasers, and he had battled long and hard with the First Lord of the Admiralty over India. As it turned out, he had no need to feel nervous, but it was understandable that he did so.

Chamberlain's fall coincided not only with the Allied withdrawal from Narvik, but with the German invasion of France. To the end Labour supported Halifax, though they also expressed a perfect willingness to work with Churchill. The crucial decision was made by Halifax himself, whom Chamberlain as well as Butler had tried to persuade to take the job. Butler was probably right when he said that Halifax was 'bent on self-abnegation', but he also made the practical point that a wartime Prime Minister in the House of Lords would find it very difficult to exercise his full authority over the House of Commons, especially with such a man as Churchill as the dominant figure in that Chamber. Churchill, as is well known, plunged into the greatest task of his life with infectious energy and enthusiasm.

Good news was already reaching Butler's ears about his personal prospects. The two principal dispensers of patronage under the Churchill régime were Lord Beaverbrook and Brendan Bracken, Churchill's faithful Irish follower. Butler heard news to the effect that Bracken liked and admired him, news which came as a surprise considering that Bracken was one of the principal figures on the tough right and had, of course, supported Churchill to the point of fanaticism and beyond both on India and on appeasement.

In any event Churchill sent for Butler and told him that he wished him to continue at the Foreign Office for the time being not least because of the exceptional subtlety and skill he had been showing in the House in answering difficult and complicated questions on foreign affairs. Butler evidently showed a certain amount of surprise at being treated thus graciously by a man who had no cause to love him, and Churchill gave him a characteristically whimsical reason for his behaviour: 'Although we have had disagreements, you once asked me to your private residence.' It would not have been easy for the Butlers to repeat the invitation for some time. They were bombed out of two homes during the German onslaught on London, and ended up staying with the Channons in Belgrave Square, a house where the gracious living made possible by considerable wealth continued throughout the war.

Butler continued at the Foreign Office, first under Halifax and then under Eden, until the summer of 1941. He got on reasonably well with Eden, and saw a good deal of the Prime Minister, helping him on one notable occasion in the garden of No.10 Downing Street to rehearse the famous phrases about fighting on the beaches and on the landing grounds. Halifax was with them on this occasion and Butler recalls that Churchill stopped sharply at one point to ask his companions if they themselves would fight in the streets and on the hills. They hastily assured him that they would, and the rehearsal went on.

But the satisfaction of foreign policy work was gone. Butler was not fitted by temperament, and was not in any case invited, to work at the sharp end of the war. As Lord Grey of Falloden, British Foreign Secretary at the outbreak of the First World War had long ago discovered, and described eloquently in his memoirs, wartime diplomacy without victory is well-nigh impossible: there was little that the Foreign Office could do except to try to keep the Americans sweet. And much of that task was handled by Halifax in Washington, by Eden and, most importantly, by Churchill himself in his long sequence of private and personal messages to Roosevelt. Much though he had enjoyed his work, therefore, Butler was vastly relieved to be summoned by Churchill and invited to become President of the Board of Education (later, the Ministry of Education). It was a job to which he had often given thought, and while one could not say he lusted after it in the way that he lusted to be Viceroy, he felt very strongly that it was a job which he could do exceptionally well; and in that he was right. He knew, moreover, that both Bracken and Gil Winant, the American Ambassador, had canvassed him for the job; Bracken went so far as to offer to get it for him at a dinner party in October 1940.

So began what was to be, and can be seen in retrospect to be, the most challenging and fulfilling part of Butler's life. He was, of course, to enjoy higher posts, and more spectacular successes, but he feels that nowhere else did he leave a legacy behind him remotely equivalent to his Education Act. A Chancellor of the Exchequer, unless he is a Pitt the Younger or a Gladstone, is rarely remembered for very long unless he makes a spectacular blunder. Leaders of the House, Home Secretaries, or even Secretaries of State for Central Africa – all posts Butler was to hold – find it peculiarly difficult, however well they discharge their jobs, to feel when their stint is over that something of historical importance has been achieved or that some enduring monument has been left behind.

From his very first day, and greatly assisted by the loyal support of his (Labour) Under-Secretary Chuter Ede and an exceptional Civil Service team, Butler set about carving his monument. As I have already mentioned he had brooded about this job and its possibilities for some time. However, I expect that an extra edge may have been provided to the knife of his ambition by a slight resentment of Churchill's obvious surprise that a young man of his abilities should so tamely have accepted a post that took him so far away from the centre where, in Churchill's view, the real work was to be done. Indeed, of their conversations on this subject which he recalls, Butler cannot remember the Prime Minister taking more than an eccentric interest in any aspect of it except the preparation – as a result of a conference in Cambridge between representatives of all the main Churches except the Roman Catholics – of a common syllabus for religious teaching.

The field of educational reform had lain fallow – with the exception of one or two spectacular rows – since the Conservative Education Act of 1902, an Act which had aroused such bitter controversy that the party was substantially damaged by the fall-out from it in the 1906 general election. Three times the Asquith government had tried to pass a major Education Bill and three times they had failed. The whole subject was rife with potential for the most serious and damaging political controversy, principally because of the involvement of the different Churches. The system was a highly complicated one but in essence the grammar schools, at the top end of the ladder of quality, were restricted to a very small number of children. The Act of 1936 had sought to improve things by raising the school-leaving age to fifteen but that proposal was, of course, killed by the outbreak of war. Various would-be reformers, in the Churches, in the TUC, in the National Union of Teachers and in politics sought by different means to achieve the desired end of providing a sound education for all children who could benefit from it. But the really serious difficulties about taking the required steps had to do both with the attitudes of the Churches and the method of financing secondary education that had grown up over the years.

Put briefly, the situation was as follows. In the nineteenth century education had been provided by voluntary bodies, and for most of that century, and into the twentieth, these had been assisted by grants from central government. Of such bodies the most important was the Church of England's National Society. The Roman Catholics were the next most influential and consequential group. Put together the Church schools educated two and a half million children and, side by side with them, educated in far fewer schools, were two and a quarter million children being taught in schools provided by the local education authorities. The whole system was in bad repair, both as to quality of teaching and provision of buildings. But while the Treasury resisted any further increase of the burden on government, public opinion bitterly resisted the idea that Church schools should be assisted from the rates, while the Catholic Church in particular resisted the idea that Catholic ratepayers and taxpayers, already generously providing for schools of their own denomination, should be required to shoulder a further burden for other than Catholic schools.

It was Butler's task both to bring home to the public and to those with influence over the system just how bad things were. In this he was greatly assisted by two things. The necessity to evacuate children from war zones, and the publicity that attended it, revealed to many who had not hitherto given the matter much or indeed any consideration just how appalling the situation was in many British schools. And then, as often happens when a nation faces the kind of great crisis that a major war involves, there suddenly grew up an urge to make a better life for the future. This instinct for change, reform and improvement, which was to lead to the election of a Labour government in 1945, burgeoned mightily in Britain from the outset of the war; and Butler made skilful and intelligent use of it, particularly in his negotiations with the Churches, though the Catholics proved obdurate to the end.

So did the Prime Minister. Although he later came to look with favour on many schemes of post-war reconstruction, the fact of the matter was that in 1941 Churchill still had the most vivid memories of the rumpus over the 1902 Act, and he was determined that Butler should not be allowed to provoke controversy. When Butler wrote to him stressing the urge for reform, and instancing in particular the need for a settlement with the Churches, the reform of religious instruction and the introduction of technical and industrial training, he replied in a hostile vein:

> It would be the greatest mistake to raise the 1902 controversy during the war, and I certainly cannot contemplate a new Education Bill. I think it would be a great mistake to stir up the public schools question at the present time. No one can possibly tell what the financial and economic state of the country will be when the war is over. Your main task at present is to get the schools working as well as possible under all the difficulties of air attack, evacuation etc. If you can add to this industrial and technical training, enabling men not required for the Army to take their places promptly in munitions industry or radio work, this would be most useful. We cannot have any party politics in wartime, and both your second and third points raise these in a most acute and dangerous form. Meanwhile you have a good scope as an administrator.

Butler took this hard, for he had come to the erroneous conclusion that his appointment had been made with reform in mind. However, aided by the sympathy of his staff, he applied himself to devising a plan and, as he says with justified pride, three years after he had received Churchill's minute he had placed a new Education Act on the statute book. How he did it remains even today a miracle of political manipulation and shows all Butler's formidable skills at their very best.

Butler decided that nothing should be done about the public schools. The other two minefields were the Churches and the area of potential political conflict. It had become necessary to acquire allies, for only if he were convinced that there was no scope for controversy could the Prime

Minister be persuaded to give his assent to any scheme that Butler might put forward. The first thing he did was to encourage the publication of a great number of reform schemes, beginning with the ministerial Green Book of 1941. This of course stimulated others, and the market was soon awash with proposals. He was well aware of the highly unequal merits of many of these ideas, but his concern was in the first instance to stimulate discussion and so to alter the general climate as to have it widely if not generally accepted that reform was required. Then it would be time enough to tackle the thorny details of the reform itself.

In a speech to the National Union of Teachers in 1942 Butler set out his own aims: elementary education up to eleven and secondary education for all after that age to be combined with a reformed system of apprenticeship with a practical form of education. And, greatly daring, he called for an end to the dual system of provided and non-provided schools, in other words for some sort of merger between Church and local authority schools. Here a diplomatic difficulty arose, even before coming to the strictly religious question of Christian teaching, involving the financial inducements he had to make available in order to transfer denominational schools to the control of local authorities. He wanted, while abolishing the existing dual system, to make a distinction between controlled and aided schools, the creation of which involved a very large shift of in particular Church of England schools into the local authority sector. A Church school, in his view, should be able to decide whether, in the future, it would be 'controlled' or 'aided'. If the former, control of the school – including financial outlay, the appointment of most teachers and even the majority of its governors – would pass to the local education authority. If, on the other hand, the school was aided, the local authority would pay salaries and running expenses, but the managers or governors would be responsible for maintaining standards and for capital improvements, towards which they would receive a fifty per cent Treasury grant. In such cases the managers – appointed by the Church authorities – would retain the right to hire and fire teachers and to insist on the exact form of religious instruction they favoured.

The fifty per cent Treasury figure was, to Butler, crucial. The object of the operation, besides procuring much greater and more efficiently deployed sums for educational investment, was to bring all schools up to standard, and to broaden both the curriculum and the achievement: he once confessed to Churchill, though it was at the time (and very largely still is) heretical for a minister to say so, that he very much wanted to influence what was actually taught in the schools of Britain; this, I think, was the teacher *manqué* coming out in him. However, the Catholics were most resistant to these reforms, and to their schools becoming controlled. They had not taken part in the Cambridge conference on an agreed religious syllabus and thus, though the Free Churches and the Anglicans could, from the strictly religious point of view, accept with equanimity the prospect of their children going to controlled schools, the Catholics could not. Given, moreover, what I have already mentioned, Catholic resentment that they had both to provide their own schools – for reasons of conscience – and, as citizens, support the other sectors, they tried all along to insist that the Exchequer grant to aided schools should amount to seventy-five per cent of expenditure.

This Butler could not accept. It was not so much a question of amount, though that, of course, was not without significance, but of likely consequence. It was crucial to his whole policy that very large numbers of Church of England schools should, with the consent of the Anglican hierarchy, enter the controlled area and the state system, and that, over the coming years a very strong temptation should exist for other declining schools to do likewise. Thus he would abolish the dual system, establish a uniform set of standards over the country and ensure – because of public involvement – that those standards would be maintained. If he dished out seventy-five per cent grants the sums would be great enough to encourage the Church schools to stay independent. Fifty per cent was a very precisely and very nicely calculated figure.

There were a great many other complications and many battles to fight, not just with Church leaders, but with many passionately committed groups within the Churches themselves. It is wonderful to read, not only in his own memoirs, but in other memoirs of the time, how Butler picked his way through the minefields. He was always available to see or visit interested parties. He was always completely briefed, patient, courteous, humorous – and even religious. He caused a certain amount of gratified surprise on one occasion when he invited Temple, the Archbishop of Canterbury, to conclude a business meeting with a prayer. And when he had a rather unsatisfactory meeting with the Catholic Archbishop Amigo of Southwark and the latter observed that had Butler been a Catholic he would have invited him to pray, the President of the Board none the less offered to join him on his knees there and then.

Here, therefore, was a subject and a challenge made for Butler's particular talents. It was vitally important, and was seen to be so by many disparate individual groups of powerful beliefs and convictions, considerable influence, and mighty commitment. It was also immensely complicated, and required for a solution the most complex balancing between different considerations and requirements. It was a subject on which, as far as the government was concerned, he could work alone; for all the Prime Minister's suspicions and fears Butler knew that if he could bring the contending forces outside Westminster if not to agreement then to something approaching compromise, he would get his Bill. Furthermore, because there were so many facets of the subject, Butler could negotiate: he could drop something here, and compromise on something there without weakening the main thrust of his policy, nor losing sight of his principal objectives.

In dealing with the Anglicans he had an easier task than with the Catholics. The Anglican hierarchy was far more united than the Catholic, which was presided over by the aged, cantankerous and failing Cardinal Hinsley. Temple of Canterbury, on the other hand, was not only a man whom Butler found congenial, but a variety of Christian Socialist. At one meeting between them Butler produced a devastating statistical indictment of Church of England schools as they stood, and the Archbishop immediately took his point. Butler knew better than to try the same line of argument with the Catholics: a much milder attempt to demonstrate the financial advantages of going along with his plans to a group of northern Catholic bishops met with the response from one that they expected their people to suffer for the faith.

That meeting took place in December 1943, and Butler felt by then that he was almost ready to act. He never did win over the Catholics, though some episcopal criticism was muted as a result of his diplomacy. Already, he had gone some way towards preparing the necessary political ground for his Bill. He had been to Chequers in the spring to talk to Churchill, partly about education, since the Prime Minister had decided to make a major speech on domestic policy which, perforce, would have to include educational references. Butler found it hard going to work with Churchill on a speech. Much later, in 1950, when it was suggested that he and Churchill together should write the Conservative election manifesto (Churchill being ambitious to write it himself and his colleagues fearing that he would let his pen run away with him), Butler demurred, pointing out wisely that the sharp contrast between their prose styles would produce so self-evident a hotch-potch that it would evoke no more than derision from the press.

On the occasion of the Chequers visit, however, Butler bent his will to the achievement of his objectives. Denied more than a brief glance at the first draft, he worked through the night on the educational section and, after a good deal of grumbling and opposition, persuaded Churchill the following morning to accept nearly all of his amendments, particularly a passage on the importance and character of religious education. If it was far from the ideal of a Prime Minister enthusiastically behind him, and well-informed about what he was doing, it was still something. In the Conservative Party then, even more so than now, aspiring advisers and ministers or shadow ministers knew the crucial significance of success in inserting one's own views – or even mention of the importance of one's own subject – in a speech by the leader. Such references attained an almost religious significance, and if it did not always follow that they procured success for the aspirant, success was unlikely without them.

After this modest triumph Butler decided to step up the pace, and in April he sent a paper on educational reconstruction to the Cabinet. In July he published his White Paper, attended by a motto from Disraeli: 'Upon the education of the people of this country the fate of this country depends.' Cabinet discussion of his memorandum on educational reconstruction was not altogether easy: a number of ministers were concerned at the public furore Butler might be about to cause. But Butler himself was satisfied, principally for the reason that the discussion made it clear that none of his proposals would have a deleterious effect on the solidarity of the National Government; all political objections were thus swept away.

Indeed, during his long period of preparation the

political climate had swung wholly Butler's way by the time he rose to speak on the second reading of his Bill in January 1944. Whatever surprises the war had left in store it was clear that the Allies were winning. Minds were thus turning with considerable celerity to the problems of post-war reconstruction. The Bill – or at least the idea of educational reform – had many well-wishers on both sides of the House, and few wanted to risk the kind of controversy that might attend open discussion of the education problem during a post-war general election. Then, again, Butler was ready on his subject, while his colleagues were not ready on theirs. The business of Parliament was languishing: the war no longer required legislation, and ministers in domestic departments had nothing prepared. Butler's foresight and determination from the very moment he had received his appointment was thus amply rewarded, when the time came, by the lavish provision of parliamentary time and the exceptional gratitude of the Whips that at least one minister was giving members something to do.

The progress of the Bill through the House of Commons – its passage in the Lords was trouble-free – gave a further opportunity to Butler to display his skills and increase his reputation: indeed he showed on this occasion many of those qualities which, years afterwards, made him such a distinguished Leader of the House. In his memoirs he tells us particularly how he constructed his speech for the Second Reading, dividing it, like a football match, into two halves, the non-contentious material in the first, the potentially controversial in the second. This was, and has remained, typical of all Butler's speech construction, and it may be convenient to digress here and consider his methods, for they are highly illustrative of his character as a politician.

Every experienced public speaker, good, bad or indifferent, knows the importance of – and probably has theories about – arranging his materials and his arguments to some extent to appeal to the susceptibilities of his audience. If, however, an orator has great power or reputation – if he is a Churchill, say, or an Enoch Powell – the tactical requirement is smaller, the argument can take the natural course of logic, and the speaker can trust either to his passion or the sheer technical quality of his speaking to overwhelm his audience. Butler, as I have observed before, has never been a great or inspiring public speaker: his style is too cerebral for that. He has always been, however, a fine parliamentary debater, because Parliament is far more susceptible to his conversational and reasonable style; he has never tried to carry a point purely by rhetoric, or by an appeal to faith. He always invokes reason, or possibility.

But he also always subjects his material and his arguments *entirely* to his conception of what the audience can be made to take. I have seen him take a draft speech (and I understand that hundreds of civil servants over the years have had the same experience) and attack it, not with a pencil or pen, but with scissors. Having sorted out the progression of the argument in his own mind, he then considers the seperate elements in the light of how he thinks the audience will react – here the popular, here the definitely unpopular, here the uncontroversial. The speech has then to be reconsidered in the light of how the audience is to be played upon. Curiously, though he has not often sought to build upon the popular things he wants to say, he will sometimes fudge the unpopular ones. I have heard him several times over the years escape with the utterance of (to the audience of the moment) the most outrageous sentiments simply because his hearers did not really understand what he was saying, or where he was leading them. Afterwards, of course, Butler would claim that he had stated his views with perfect clarity, and that they had gained acceptance; but the activity, so often repeated, did, over the years, contribute towards his reputation for slipperiness.

The technique reflects what amounts on Butler's part not just to a tactical or cynical belief in politics as the art of the possible, but a belief that is fundamental to his moral nature. If he can he will resort to procedural or tactical or stylistic tricks to gain a point. Thus, to avoid the danger of a discussion of the role of public schools in 1944, he referred the whole question to the Fleming Committee, ensuring that it would not report before the Bill had been passed. To avoid as far as possible rows over the absorption of the so-called 'Part III' authorities (those in charge of elementary schools only), he put the provisions regarding them into a Schedule to the Bill, thus avoiding potentially damaging debate at an early stage. But if such manoeuvres are not possible Butler has been invariably prepared to give up what he wanted in the first place. He has convictions – many, and strongly held – but no conviction that he has ever had has seemed to him to be, in his political life, an overriding matter of principle; he has been content in his work as in his oratory to settle for what he can get.

This is illustrated, not merely by what happened at the one major crisis of the Bill's passage, but by his comment on it. The situation was this. By 1944 there was considerable agitation on the subject of equal pay for women, especially in the Civil Service, and in the teaching profession. A band of Tory rebels (Quintin Hogg was among them, but their intellectual leader was Thelma Cazalet) decided to seek in committee to amend the clause dealing with pay in favour of women, and in this they were supported by the Labour members. Because the Bill's progress had been steady, and even uneventful, the Whips were relaxed, and the government went down to defeat by one vote.

The implications of this defeat were important. The government was simply not prepared, at this time, to consider the question of equal pay, both because of cost and because of the considerable administrative upheaval it would cause. But if the amended clause was allowed to stand an important precedent would have been created, and it might well have been impossible to avoid facing the general question, with consequences of unknown import. Butler – on this rare occasion losing his normal imperturbability – was furious. It was not that he was against equal pay: on this, as on many other issues, he was always in the van of enlightenment. But he took the view that the rebels were now endangering his whole Bill, and inserting a matter of general policy which should be dealt with (as it eventually was) by quite seperate legislation, into a Bill solely and specifically concerned with education. He went to see Churchill.

The upshot of the matter was that the Prime Minister decided to make the restoration of the original clause a matter of confidence: if the government lost, therefore, it would be immediately necessary to hold a general election. And Butler received support from many other, and often quite unexpected, sources: Ernest Bevin said that if Butler was forced out of office he would go too. Bevin's promise – or threat – arose from a belief that very rapidly gained currency, and has been repeated over the years since. This belief was that Butler, seeing the potentially enormous damage the amended clause might do to his Bill, threatened to resign if the original was not restored in full. The belief was immensely beneficial to his reputation: it presented him as a strong, decided, committed and even powerful political leader, able to persuade even Churchill to lay the life of his government on the line for the sake of the Education Bill.

But Butler declined to accept at the time, and has always declined to accept, the almost heroic role thus thrust upon him. According to his account it was the Prime Minister who decided to make the issue one of confidence, and for reasons that had nothing whatever to do with education. The House of Commons had become slack, Churchill declaimed. The House had forgotten there was a war on. He was going to 'rub the rebels' noses in their mess'. He did so, and the clause was restored with a massive majority producing, besides, the incidental but useful benefit that nobody thereafter dared to press an amendment that was unacceptable to the government, and so even the controversial abolition of Part III authorities passed through without difficulty. This is an entirely convincing account, and it is both characteristic and admirable of Butler that he should always have refused to accept a reputation he did not deserve.

Butler was not then, and never has been since, uncritical of his brainchild, for all his considerable pride in laying the keel of the modern British educational system. He never expected his Act to last forever and believed, indeed, that the impossibility of getting a final settlement on the nature of the system through Parliament at that time meant that there would have to be a good deal of change as the years passed. What has distressed him from time to time has been that the efforts he made to build flexibility into the Act, to allow for change and improvement and development, have so often failed because succeeding ministers and governments have not shared his vision. Thus, for example, more than once during the passage of the Bill he forecast the gradual melding, at least in some parts of the country, of the grammar and secondary modern schools into a comprehensive system. It is the very evident failings of the comprehensive system as it exists today, and their loathing of it, that makes numbers of Conservatives nowadays look back with dissatisfaction and bitterness on the 1944 Act. Butler's reply to this I find entirely convincing. What hindered the gradual evolution he foresaw and intended, he says, what damaged the system itself and incited criticism of it, was the decision of successive Labour ministers and local authorities to make of the development of comprehensive schools a matter of doctrine rather than of empirical management. Doctrine in politics is in any event anathema to him; and it is particularly so in an area of political activity where his own achievements were so striking. As

Churchill telegraphed him after the Bill had received the Royal Assent: 'You have added a notable Act to the Statute Book and won a lasting place in the history of British Education'.

These labours completed there was little more for Butler to do in the immediate future. Like Churchill himself he hoped very much that the National Government could be kept in being, at least until the war against Japan was won, but perhaps even until the social welfare legislation that had been agreed upon in committees of all three parties could be enacted. But Labour would have none of it and, besides, despite the drastic wartime decline of the Conservative Party's legendary organization, the majority of Conservatives were in a buoyant and even bellicose mood in the face of a general election; with Churchill at their head, they felt, they could not lose. Churchill, depressed though he was, as he put it, at the prospect of declining from being a national to a mere party leader, was rather of their mind, and ran a campaign of unexampled aggression. It was a complete failure not, Butler thinks, simply because of its crudity, but because everything the Tories had to advocate was out of tune with the mood of post-war Britain. The Labour victory did not surprise him. He had long predicted it. All that took him aback, as it did many others, was its extent.

So, at last, Labour entered into the heritage for which it had so long worked. 'My present feeling', James Stuart, the then Conservative Chief Whip, wrote to Butler, 'is not so much one of depression as of waking up in a world completely strange to me. I feel that my entrails have been pulled right out of me.' It was a common feeling among Tories, and Churchill for some time shared it. Butler, if not exactly made of sterner stuff, was at least to some extent cushioned by the fact that he had seen defeat coming. He did not think then, and he does not think now, that there was any way to save the Conservative Party in 1945, given the hated memories of the thirties and the bright, shining promise of the new Labour doctrines, carried and enforced with enthusiasm and fire. Besides, there was already a new task he had set himself: to remake his party.

5

The New Conservatives

Churchill formed an interim government for the brief period between the break-up of the Coalition and the Labour victory. In it Butler served as Minister of Labour; it was a few weeks of no great significance in his life, save that it contributes to his extraordinary record for variety of offices held. Now, in 1945, he was for the first time in his political career in opposition.

Politicians vary in their capacity to perform in opposition. Some (Harold Wilson was a good example) enjoy it, and are far more effective there than in government. Others (Edward Heath is the prime recent example) are wretched, both in themselves and in their performance. Butler was statesmanlike. Because Churchill ran his front bench on a very loose rein (there was, in those days, nothing like the elaborate formal structure of shadow Cabinets and supporting front-bench spokesmen we have in opposition today) Butler was able to speak on a variety of subjects – India, foreign affairs and education among them – in which he had had experience in the previous twelve years.

Moreover, particularly once the Labour Foreign Secretary, Ernest Bevin, abandoned his conciliatory attitude to Soviet Russia and began to concentrate on supporting the United Nations effort in Korea, the alliance with the United States and the forging of NATO, Butler found himself able to offer constructive opposition, rather than the tooth and claw stuff that Churchill, and a number of his other colleagues, favoured.

This was entirely in tune with his temperament. I doubt if he would ever have been happy with that guerrilla warfare which is an essential part of, but never should become the whole of, any mode of parliamentary opposition. He did not have the talent, nor the guts, nor the inclination for it. It suited him admirably to continue building up his reputation as an increasingly senior and wise political figure in the counsels of the nation and, moreover, one who had the wisdom and charity to see the good points in what the Attlee government was trying to achieve. Like Churchill, he regretted the Edwardian days during which, however vicious politicians were about one another in public, they could and would, even when they came from different parties, remain on good private and social terms. It was not so easy in 1945, he thought, partly because the intellectual conviction of Labour members and the size of their majority made them arrogant, partly because there was a social gulf between the two parties in the post-war period which had not existed when Churchill was a young man. So, not only in his contributions to debate, but in other ways as well, Butler sought to create civilized relations between members from both parties and, as time went by, a thaw set in in their relations with one another.

The years in opposition did a good deal to solidify the reputation Butler had gained as a parliamentarian with the Education Act. He worked exceptionally hard: it will be seen just how hard when we discuss the detail of his contribution to the making of new party policy. He spoke on a great variety of subjects, never less than well, and always well-prepared. He was forty-three, a mere stripling as judged in terms of that political era. But gradually he drew around him that mantle of aged agelessness which, in the fifties, was so vital a part of his political image. By the time the Conservatives returned to power in 1951 nobody but himself doubted that he was entitled to and would receive a post of the highest seniority.

Butler, who through his in-laws, the Courtaulds, had any number of opportunities to do what most senior Tories do in opposition, and go into the City (though Churchill only ever took one directorship) eschewed all such temptations in favour of a completely full-time political career. Of that period, but particularly of his work at the Conservative Research Department and the Conservative Political Centre, he writes: 'I enjoyed the period so much that I had little time to worry about personal ambition, though I clearly saw that a fine opportunity had been given me to render service to the Party.'

He began work over breakfast at home, and divided morning, afternoon and evening between Old Queen Street, the House of Commons and speaking engagements in the country. The days and the weeks were full and, to him, utterly absorbing. The wide variety of his parliamentary contributions, and the opportunity the research work he presided over gave him to learn about many problems which he had never touched before, both ministered to his hunger for ordered knowledge and satisfied his pedagogical instincts. Probably the only shadow over his life, and this did not come until later in the period that stretches for ten years from 1945 to 1955 and the succession of Eden, was the declining health of his beloved wife Sydney, who died in 1952.

The origins of Butler's dominant involvement in post-war Conservative planning – apart from his own wishes –

lay in Churchill's reluctant appointment, in 1941, of a Party Committee on Post-war Problems, among the luminaries of which were Butler himself and David Maxwell-Fyfe, subsequently Lord Kilmuir, and Lord Chancellor. The work done between 1941 and the end of the war was necessarily intermittent and patchy; but at least some work was being done, and the men doing it had the liveliest appreciation of the necessity of putting the whole business on a much more developed footing after peace returned, a feeling strengthened in most quarters when Churchill went down to electoral defeat.

Butler found himself, after the dust of the election defeat had settled down, in charge of three interlocking operations of great potential and increasing importance. The first – and, in essence, the bedrock of the whole enterprise – was the Conservative Research Department (CRD), which I discussed in part in Chapter 1. The second was the Conservative Political Centre (CPC). The CPC, which exists and flourishes to this day, lived a separate administrative life from the CRD. It was concerned with publishing, propaganda and education, and was formed on the model of the Fabian Society; but it drew, of course, a great deal on the CRD, some of whose members wrote some of its most distinguished pamphlets. The third was the Industrial Policy Committee, the principal purpose of which was to draft the first and most famous of the Butler charters: the Industrial Charter. The Committee did not have a separate administrative existence; it met in Old Queen Street and was attended by the then Director of the department, David Clarke, and some of his brightest young men. But it had an outside membership, consisting of some important and imaginative Tory industrialists and businessmen whose support for its aims and hard work for its success gave it weight and, in the end, great influence.

Churchill was highly suspicious of all this intellectualizing. He had the profoundest fear of an opposition spelling out its policy in too much detail, both for fear of giving hostages to fortune when power was regained, and because he saw the dangers of the government, once the opposition had published something detailed, using the resources available to it to smash those proposals in a propaganda campaign. Butler and others won him over to the idea that some serious rethinking was necessary and that the party had to come to terms somehow with the new world which the war and the Labour triumph had created. He went along with that but even so Butler followed his orders in never allowing published proposals to become too embedded in detail. And it is clear that Churchill never gave specific permission for the Industrial Charter to be published in 1947. He merely, just before instructions to print had to be given, entertained Butler to a lavish lunch and praised him highly. Butler took this to be permission.

Apart from the remoteness, even suspicion, of Churchill, Butler had other problems to face. There was the problem of making his often headstrong young team at the CRD work together. There was also the opposition of the party's right wing to what he was doing: 'pink socialism' was one of the more polite epithets applied to his work. And there was conscious friction between the CRD and the Conservative Central Office under its formidable Chairman, Lord Woolton. In his own, in general unrevealing, memoirs Woolton wrote caustically about the set-up he found in the party: having observed that the CRD was 'under the personal control of Mr R.A. Butler', he adds:

> The Conservative Political Centre, which was the mouth-piece of the Research Department, again was independent of the Central Office except when the bills came in. The Central Office had its own propaganda department, but there was no connection between them and the Political Centre except through the Chairman of the Party.

At one stage, however, Butler was moved to put the matter the other way round: he felt impelled to write to Woolton gently to complain about the fact that Central Office was giving insufficient publicity to the work of the CRD and the Industrial Policy Committee.

Butler says of his CRD team:

> I was looking for people with great intelligence and constructive minds, essentially alert and preferably young. But they did not have to be from the same mould. Individual flair, imagination and even idiosyncrasy were to be encouraged, provided all concerned remained loyal to the party and did not go into rebellion on a major issue. Because we followed the middle way we were at times attacked from our left as well as from our right; but one of the abiding assets of the Conservative Party is its flexibility – it can absorb a wide discrepancy of views among its members and still remain a coherent and unified entity.

There can be no doubt that Butler assembled an extraordinary galaxy of talent, not only in full-time jobs but on his Industrial Policy Committee. It requires a genuine effort of mind to recall that, though they were older than the average CRD intake today, Maudling, Macleod and Powell were junior stars in his firmament. It was the team he assembled – including those like Lyttelton, Stanley, Macmillan and Maxwell-Fyfe who were professional politicians rather than backroom boys – that re-made the Conservative Party and laid the foundations of the 1951 election victory.

Churchill's tolerance was essential to the enterprise, but the great man himself was not precisely the opposition leader that such as Butler could have wished for. His energy, attention, and real interest were centred on the stage that he had occupied for so long – that of international affairs. His international, and, for that matter, his domestic political reputation had suffered not at all from his defeat, as he realized once he had recovered from the initial shock. (It was described by his wife as 'a blessing in disguise', to which he replied that it was a blessing very well disguised indeed!) His concern with economic and domestic policy was fitful and haphazard; he trusted to the swings and roundabouts to bring him back to office in due course. The astonishing fires of energy that had sustained him in the war, and particularly in its first years, had burned low. He was seized – as he was until the very moment that he retired as Prime Minister – with the feeling that he still had one great last contribution to make, not to his country so much as to the world, and to peace. Thus his time as leader of the opposition is remembered principally for the great speech at Fulton, Missouri, on the Iron Curtain, not for any particular contribution to the rejuvenation of the Conservative Party. That work, even allowing for the help of many skilled hands, was Butler's. Eden, the designated successor of the war leader, approved of what Butler was doing and, in general, took a liberal line in domestic affairs. But he had had absolutely no experience of any home department, and he never had more than a cursory interest in domestic affairs. For good or ill, and with its failings as well as its strengths, the Conservative Party that came to power in 1951 and stayed there for thirteen years was Butler's creation.

And yet it is hard to be precisely clear about what changes of a fundamental nature Butler made. He rigidly observed Churchill's injunction not to be too specific, principally in the preparation of the Industrial Charter, but also in the writing and publishing of the many other policy documents that flowed from the CRD and the CPC in an increasing stream as the general election came closer. The party was to be given a human face, as it were. It was to be shown to be, not the stupid party, but one whose leaders were fully as intelligent and as up to the minute as those of the Labour Party. It was no longer to be a fully capitalist, *laissez-faire* organization, but then, it never has been, as Butler himself rightly stresses. To see the Tories of the late twenties and early thirties as such – as a large part of the electorate of 1945 undoubtedly did see them – was a travesty of historical truth. Within the limits of the times Neville Chamberlain was probably the best, as he was certainly the most efficient, minister in charge of health and local government that the country has ever had. Certainly, in the grim years of the thirties, Harold Macmillan, supported by a handful of Tory friends, advocated a far more left-wing social and economic policy than Baldwin or Chamberlain would think of accepting, and Macmillan, at one stage, resigned the Conservative Whip in despair; but at that time Macmillan's views were scarcely distinguishable from those of the socialists.

Later, when Butler was Chancellor of the Exchequer and Hugh Gaitskell his shadow, the *Economist* coined the term 'Butskellism' to indicate the measure of economic agreement that existed between the two men. Butler objects to the word, and he emphasizes (what it is unfashionable to say in the current travails of the Labour Party) how thoroughgoing a socialist Gaitskell was, as left-wing, certainly, as Tony Benn is today (except on matters of defence policy) but eschewing a left-wing style. It is true, however, that, as the swollen heads of the Labour majority of 1945 reduced in size under the combined pressures of events, bad luck and the atmosphere of the House of Commons, there was a certain growing together, the positive quality of which was emphasized by the various rebellions within the Labour Party of Aneurin Bevan. I have already quoted Butler's remark to the effect that differences of wealth and style of life made intimacy between government and opposition after 1945 much less easy than it had been before; but he also stresses that the Labour leaders were, in general, middle-class intellectuals dissatisfied with the political implications of their upbringing. They were not revolutionaries, because they had too much to lose. The reforms on which they had set their hearts, once accomplished – principal among them the introduction of the welfare state – their approach to change in society became more gradualist.

This gradualism became more marked through the long ascendancy of the Conservative Party in the fifties; just as Butler had been determined in 1945 that the Conservative Party had to shift to the left both in policy and style to imitate Labour, so, in the fifties, Labour shifted to the right. Gaitskell's attempt to drop his party's commitment to far-reaching nationalization, and Antony Crosland's books arguing the same point, were the mirror image of what Butler had done in Old Queen Street. Until very recently it has been the rule in British politics that opposition imitates government, if only as a means of finding out what particular trick it is the other lot have mastered so well as to get them into power. Butler heartily approves of this process, and hence applauds himself for the statesmanlike line he took in post-1945 debates. His approval he emphasizes heavily in his memoirs, and he has certainly been uneasy in the years since Edward Heath's election as Conservative leader in 1965 at both the extent to which the two major parties have diverged and the fact that the experience of opposition has moved the Tories to the right and Labour to the left. This wider divergence is changing the nature of British political culture and Butler, from a much older school, regards the spectacle with a good deal of unease, as is demonstrated by his opposition in the House of Lords to certain of Mrs Thatcher's government's proposals, for example, to charge for school transport.

Carefully calibrated by Butler, the presentation as well as the preparation of the new Conservatism built up momentum steadily between the general election of 1945 and that of 1950. On 11 May 1947 the Industrial Charter appeared; only on the right and the left among the newspapers was it ill-received. Within the party Eden, in particular, lent the document powerful public support. At the party conference in Brighton only three members of an audience of four thousand raised dissenting voices against its adoption as party policy. Butler now went full steam ahead: charters appeared on the subjects of Welsh and Scottish affairs, on agriculture and on other subjects, while there appeared to be an unending stream of cogent, stylish and reformist pamphlets materializing from the CPC.

Meanwhile, Butler had made another important innovation. This was the creation, under the aegis of the CPC, of the so-called two-way movement of ideas, which is to this day an important part of Tory organization. It works in this way: the CRD and the CPC prepare briefing documents on a topic of the moment. These – invariably elegantly printed – are circulated to a vast number of CPC groups throughout the country, and discussed at local meetings. A summary of each of these proceedings is returned to the centre, and digested by the party's research staff. A report is then prepared which goes both to the leadership and back to the grassroots. Nor is there anything about this exercise that is merely window dressing: in my own time at the CRD I saw a number of significant changes of policy or of emphasis within policy made as a result of this kind of elaborate research. And for all that the partisans of the other two British political parties vaunt their own ideas of participatory democracy as against the authoritarianism of the Conservatives, neither of them has ever created any system for the exchange and development of ideas remotely as sophisticated or as wide-ranging as this.

After the Brighton Conference of 1947 Butler gradually began to get his way against the indifference, sometimes amounting to hostility, of Lord Woolton to the kind of propaganda the CRD and CPC wanted. After the 1945 defeat the party, and especially its leadership, had become acutely aware of the fact that the legendary Tory election machine had, quite simply, ceased to exist; during the war Labour had kept its local machines intact, the Conservatives had let theirs go. Thus it was that Butler's old ally on the Post-war Problems Committee, David Maxwell-Fyfe, was appointed to head a committee of inquiry into the state of the party. Probably most important among his many recommendations was a proposal limiting the amount of money a candidate could contribute to his local association; this greatly broadened the range of candidates available. But he also advised the reconstruction of the Advisory Committee on Policy and Political Education and this committee – though, to Butler's regret, it lost control of the CPC – meshed the whole intellectual effort of the new Conservatism into the party machine itself. Henceforth, there was much more propaganda and sales muscle behind the new ideas.

The time was rapidly approaching when all this effort had to be translated into the simpler form of propaganda which can be used to appeal to a broad public during an election campaign. Again, Butler and his men were not wanting. The 1949 conference accepted the policy document *The Right Road for Britain* – the first time that the word 'right' in both its meanings was used effectively and subtly in this way (it has never since left the Tory mind, as Mrs Margaret Thatcher's opposition document *The Right Approach* demonstrated). *The Right Road* was plagiarized for *This is the Road*, the manifesto which served, with small changes, for the elections of both 1950 and 1951, when Churchill was returned to power.

No one can ever say with absolute certainty what it is that wins elections. All retrospective analysis is based on the fact of the result, and on hindsight and on special pleading. By 1950 the Labour government was falling apart. Illnesses which proved fatal took Cripps and Bevin out of politics. Senior ministers who had been serving in high places since 1940 were exhausted. Brighter sparks like Aneurin Bevan and Harold Wilson had resigned *pour reculer mieux sauter*. The Korean war, grave economic problems, and troubles in Africa all sapped energy, and it was probably not without a certain amount of relief that Attlee, heavily battered by the opposition during the 1950 Parliament, finally laid down his burden. But if all this decay was highly advantageous to the Tories it must also be said that the team Churchill took with him to office in 1951 was the spearhead of a very different party from the one that went down to defeat in 1945. And in so far as it was a different party, and that its difference was an important fact in winning the election – as I believe it was – then the hand and the brain behind the victory were Butler's.

It was fashionable, in the boom-time of the second half of the fifties, and even in the sixties, to deride Churchill's last government as a lame-duck affair, and many historians still believe that the Prime Minister stayed far too long in office: he did not retire until April 1955, and thereafter went rapidly downhill. The strain of his long wait certainly told on Eden's always slightly unstable nerves. Churchill certainly no longer had the physical or intellectual energy to drive government on that he had had in 1940. Until the end he kept a number of ministers (and appointed others, such as Lord Alexander as Defence Minister) who were either old cronies or chums from the war; and too little effort was made (save in the striking and imaginative appointment of Iain Macleod as Minister for Health) to bring in new blood. However, the successive British crises of the sixties and seventies, together with the work of a distinguished group of young historians, especially Anthony Seldon, whose study of the 1951 government appears in 1981, has produced the beginnings of a revaluation. I have had the opportunity of looking at some of Mr Seldon's work and it certainly bears out the defence outlined in

Butler's own memoirs. In summary, the argument goes that this was probably the best-run and most efficient government Britain has had since the war. To judge it by contemporary standards – and particularly to judge its economic policy – is to emphasize that, of all post-war governments, it took the smallest percentage of the citizen's income in tax, abolished, finally, all wartime controls (the slogan for this was the famous 'Set the people free', which Mrs Thatcher used again to considerable effect in 1979), built the then unbelievable number of 300,000 houses annually and began the revival of British industry. This was done, moreover, in the face of exceptionally unfavourable international economic trends. Although the bugbear of inflation, which has ravaged the country since, was beginning to show itself by the time Butler left the Exchequer in 1955, the fact that it was not dealt with promptly was in large part the result of the collapse of the Eden government and the entry into office of Harold Macmillan, who believed in inflating the economy in order to defeat unemployment, as Edward Heath did after him.

Butler, of course, expected high office, but he had not dreamt how munificent his reward for all his work in opposition might be, for, like most politicians and commentators, he had long decided that the Treasury was marked down for Oliver Lyttelton. On being summoned to see Churchill Butler was merely passed a piece of paper with the names of the principal appointees and their departments written on it. Butler demurred slightly: Gaitskell, who had briefly been Chancellor in the Attlee government, would undoubtedly be his shadow in the House of Commons, and Gaitskell was a formidable economist. Butler had neither business nor economic experience; indeed, he had denied himself the former in order assiduously to pursue his work of policy re-formulation. But Churchill was determined. 'I have thought much about this offer,' he said, 'and in the end Anthony and I agreed that you would be best at handling the Commons.' Butler was not able to gather around him quite the team he wanted: he succeeded in bringing in Arthur Salter (though the relationship was never to prove really happy), but he failed to acquire Selwyn Lloyd as Financial Secretary, because Lloyd, who had helped enormously at the CRD, was already committed to Eden at the Foreign Office. So, not without trepidation, but confident that he had the right ideas, Butler set out to handle the toughest and most important job in the new administration.

Opinions on Butler's tenure at Great George Street still differ. He entered office to face a staggering range and number of problems, of which the most immediate and deadly was the sky-rocketing of imports into Britain: he cut back savagely by means of import controls. By the time of his 1953 and 1954 budgets he was riding the crest of a wave of success. Taxes were down. Allowances were up. Trade was reviving. The condition of the people was everywhere improving. He was handling the extremely complicated business of running both a monetary and a fiscal policy with assurance and aplomb, and he was – as Churchill had predicted he would be – master of the House of Commons. In 1955, however, he was compelled, because of the deteriorating situation, to introduce two budgets, and to throttle back the economy. It was at this stage that Eden decided to reconstruct his government, and Butler became Leader of the House of Commons. He was, at that stage, tired, for the Treasury is a most exacting job. Moreover, his beloved wife had died and his own health was by no means as robust as in the past: in 1956 a nagging virus which refused to respond to treatment kept him out of the early deliberations over the Suez crisis. Still, he was reluctant to go just then, being characteristically convinced that, having enjoyed the glory of the great days of abolishing controls and setting the economy free he should not appear to shirk hard times ahead. But Eden was determined, not least because, having proved his popularity by an unexpectedly easy general election victory in 1955, he wanted a government of his own, not one inherited from Churchill.

There is no doubt that Butler proved himself a master of the tactics of economic and budgetary policy. He was greatly helped, as Macmillan was at Housing, by enjoying Churchill's unstinting support on nearly every major issue – although on one vital matter, as we shall shortly see, that support was lacking – and, indeed, it was characteristic of Churchill's approach to government in this last period of his active life that he concentrated on a very few issues and ministers, and then applied his enormous prestige to see that the right side won. However, when Butler left the Treasury there was no monument, such as the Education Act, to leave behind. Yet there might have been and, with frankness rare in a major politician, Butler says as much in his memoirs.

The situtation was this, as Butler puts it:

> The Commonwealth Finance Ministers' Conference which had met in London in January under my chairmanship had declared the ultimate goal of the sterling area to be the convertibility of the pound. Since then rumours had been rife that I wished at the time of the Budget to make the pound convertible to non-residents at a floating rate of exchange. These rumours were well-founded. But they inevitably weakened the reserves, and when the Budget was seen to contain no proposals to this end the reverses were correspondingly strengthened.

And he comments:

> In the long-term, however, I believe that the decision not to free the pound was a fundamental mistake. The absence of a floating rate of exchange robbed successive

> Chancellors of an external regulator for the balance of payments corresponding to the internal regulator provided principally by Bank rate. If such a regulator had existed, and a floating rate been accepted, Conservatives would have been saved some of the uncertainties and indignities of 'stop-go' economics and Socialists the traumatic experience of a second formal devaluation.

The situation Butler was in was one of exceptional and acute difficulty. The principle of a fixed exchange rate was fundamental to Keynesian and old-fashioned economists alike. To the former it was necessary for the stabilization of international trade and the indispensable foundation for the eventual and visionary creation of an international unit of exchange which would ultimately provide funds for the development of poorer areas of the world. To the latter a floating rate was inherently unstable: it would create uncertainty in the markets, damage the reserves, and make orderly international trade impossible. Moreover, to float was – or would have been at the time – in effect to devalue. Conservatives were determined not to do this, for one of the heaviest sticks they had used to beat the Attlee government was the Cripps' devaluation of sterling, an unavoidable step which the opposition castigated none the less, as evidence of unsound economic management and, even, of lack of patriotism. The fixed rate was in the early fifties, and remained for many years, not just a symbol of political virility but an ark of the covenant of patriotism as well. As Butler says, the effect of all this was far-reaching: the long resistance of the first two governments led by Harold Wilson to an inevitable devaluation threw his government entirely off the rails; and the reason for the resistance was based less on economic argument than on a mulish determination not to put Wilson and his Chancellor, James Callaghan, in the same position of being pilloried by the Tories as Cripps had been. Finally, when Edward Heath was faced with a very similar position he and his

Chancellor, Lord Barber, decided to float. The intellectual climate was far more propitious for them because, not least through the public advocacy of Enoch Powell, the idea of floating rates had gained a measure of currency. However, I believe that Heath and Barber took the line they did less because they were sure it was economically right than because they and the Cabinet were determined not to allow it to be said of them that they had been forced into the same humiliating position as Cripps and Callaghan: the shibboleths remained strong. It is now, of course, very difficult, if not impossible, to conceive of a British government returning to fixed rates; hence the decision of successive governments to stay out of all arrangements by the EEC nations to fix the value of their currencies in relation to one another. As Enoch Powell said, in mockery of the dire warnings from many quarters that preceded the Heath float, 'The Treasury floated the pound, and the world did not end.'

That brief history is sufficient to indicate the kind of opposition Butler faced in 1951. Out of the entire Cabinet only Oliver Lyttelton supported him, though Lyttelton did so with enthusiasm and loyalty. He was bitterly opposed particularly by Lord Cherwell, perhaps Churchill's closest adviser. Arthur Salter, even, was against him, though he had a good deal of support in the Treasury.

So, the question is, could Butler still have won the day? It is a question that is very difficult to answer, though I think it fair to say that he might have made a stronger and better fight for a policy which, after all, he says he regarded, even then, as fundamental (as I think it was). He had some excellent cards. Despite the advocacy of Cherwell, Churchill was instinctively in favour of the float, though he admitted that he did not understand the issue fully. It seemed to his quick imagination to be all of a piece with the general policy of setting the economy and the people free; and Butler also believed this. Then again, Butler's position was far more powerful than he seems to have realized: in almost every Cabinet the Chancellor is, in domestic policy, second only to the Prime Minister, just as the Treasury is easily the most powerful department of state. The Chancellor first appointed is just as powerful in the early stages of the life of a new government as that government itself is in relation to the nation: the honeymoon period is *the* period for getting new or radical things done. However, once he saw the nature of the opposition Butler let the matter go.

Like other great turning points in his career which I have already discussed, this is one which exhibits all of Butler's essential characteristics. There is, in adopting the idea of a floating exchange rate in the face of heavy intellectual as well as practical opposition, the natural creativity, the boldness of mind of the man. In giving way without a fight we can see the equally natural timidity, the adamant attachment to the art of the possible, that is equally fundamental to his nature. He saw with absolute clarity what needed to be done. He was prepared to defend it to the death against what he knew would be the ferocious opposition of Gaitskell and the Labour Party, and even in the councils of the international economic world, where the policy was regarded with deep suspicion even by Britain's friends. But within the government and within the Conservative Party he would not fight settled opposition, and thus his legacy as Chancellor was far more limited that it need have been.

However, Butler was more important in the life of the Churchill government than even the exalted office he held, and the vital task with which he was entrusted would imply. It is extraordinary, considering the ease with which Macmillan triumphed over him in the fight for the premiership in 1957, how rapidly his career advanced in those years compared to that of Macmillan. True, Macmillan was prodigiously successful at the Ministry of Housing, particularly in keeping the promise – extorted by an enthusiastic party conference from a very unwilling front bench – to build 300,000 houses a year. Macmillan was also close to the inner Churchill circle: indeed, when asked his advice on who should succeed Eden Churchill plumped for Macmillan.

Nevertheless, in the life of the 1951 government is was Butler's star which waxed. Churchill's health was declining, and he suffered a series of strokes and arterial spasms. Eden's health had always been uncertain, and he suffered long periods of illness and convalescence. Butler was always standing by to pick up the pieces. At the time in 1953 that James Stuart, then at the Scottish Office, wrote to him, he was Chancellor, Acting Prime Minister and Acting Foreign Secretary. 'You seem well', Stuart added, ' – and I hope you are – but do please remember that you mustn't break the main spring. It takes ages to mend.' In his diary for 8 August 1953 Moran wrote perceptively of Butler at this very high point in his professional life:

> Butler, like an Asquith, is rather too impatient with pedestrian folk. He has more staying power than Anthony, but at present he lacks what people call the 'common touch'. They complain, too, that he will back a horse both ways. He seems none the worse for the grind while the P.M. and Anthony were away ill. Of course, he is aware of the danger of racing the engine, but he says he has 'a normal family life and does not feel the strain'.

There seems little doubt, therefore, that even at this climactic moment, when he was discharging so many jobs so efficiently, and when he was behaving with the utmost loyalty – in particular by urging the claims of Eden and Churchill – that the shadow of suspicion that has never left him clung around Butler. We do not fully know, of course, precisely what considerations moved Churchill in recommending Macmillan instead of him in 1957, but to put the matter in purely human terms – and that, of course, is to miss an often essential dimension in discussing public affairs – it seems that Butler was singularly ill-requited by both Churchill and Eden when his first great opportunity to be Prime Minister came his way.

More than one of Butler's friends thought he was ill-advised to accept the Leadership of the House in place of the Treasury. As before and after he hankered after the Foreign Office. But Eden was determined that that high post was a reward already earned by his Minister of State, Selwyn Lloyd, and it was not available to Butler. The Chancellorship is a difficult job to follow; after it almost anything except the Foreign Office seems to be a demotion, though as James Callaghan's career has demonstrated the demotion need not be the final chapter of a career. But the Leader of the House – whose job is both to get the government's business through and to protect the interests of all members, including those on the other side – does not have a large executive department at his back. He has a senior and dignified position, and every government badly needs a kind, and popular, Leader. But he does not have that powerful, loyal and, above all, ready support enjoyed by the heads of the larger departments both in Cabinet squabbles and in furthering their personal positions. Today Butler is rueful about accepting his fate at Eden's hands. The decline in authority which he accepted should not, he says, be in the nature of things: after all, the Leader has none of the burdens of a large department. He should be able to wander freely across the field, and influence many aspects of government policy. But that was not the way it turned out for Butler.

1955 was therefore, in some respects, the peak of Butler's career. He still had great services to perform, and considerable success to enjoy. But it is as though, at this point, the chain snapped. He had ridden upwards effortlessly from his entry into the House of Commons in 1933. He had, almost from the beginning, been at or near the centre of affairs, gaining steadily in power, prestige and experience. But in the next year the doubt about him began to accumulate, and for the first time he began to suffer a series of reverses. He took everything, as one might expect, with the utmost equanimity. He never refused a task however disagreeable it might seem, or however dangerous for himself personally he or his friends might think it to be. For the most part in public he kept his own counsel, and his doubts, reservations and criticisms of his colleagues, of that biting character discussed in earlier chapters, were kept mainly for private consumption. With his departure from the Treasury we enter the last phase of his extraordinary political life.

6
Many Hats

Apologizing to Butler, or at least explaining his decision to recommend Macmillan in 1957, Churchill later said that he had decided to cast his vote for the older man. Macmillan himself, in the only conversation about his successor as Prime Minister that Butler can recall them having, said that Butler was already too old to succeed in the sixties, and should content himself therefore with being kingmaker. This Butler naturally resented, being nine years younger than Macmillan; he would therefore, had he succeeded in the early sixties, been younger than Macmillan was at the time of his succession. However, although Butler's hopes did not truly die until the defeat at Home's hands in 1963, his fortune was withering on the vine from 1955.

The uninformed observer might well have thought the opposite. During Eden's illness after the Suez invasion Butler again found himself as Acting Prime Minister. In spite of asking for, and being denied, the Foreign Office by Macmillan, he continued to enjoy a staggering range of responsibilities. He remained Leader of the House of

Commons until 1961. From 1957 to 1962 he was Home Secretary. He was Chairman of the Conservative Party from 1959 to 1961. He enjoyed a brief stint, while winding up the Federation of Central Africa (the two Rhodesias and Nyasaland), as Secretary of State for Central African Affairs, and was designated Deputy Prime Minister from July 1962 to October 1963, this post being, as he says, one that should neither be created nor accepted. And he ended his career, under Home, as Secretary of State for Foreign Affairs. This last period, therefore, might in one light be regarded as the full flowering of his career: during it he held more posts of greater seniority than he had held throughout his earlier, and already varied, career. Even so, there was a canker already eating away at his prospects, and it could have been arrested only by the application of an utterly ruthless and determined ambition of a kind that was foreign to him.

If Butler had reservations about Anthony Eden's character and stability, and if he believed, especially after his own experience as Acting Prime Minister in 1953, that he would himself have been a better choice to succeed Churchill, he kept such beliefs to himself. That was well-advised for even though Churchill himself had grave reservations about Eden – and was not too completely surprised by the catastrophe of 1956 – the Foreign Secretary had been waiting too long in the wings, had been wearing the mantle of Heir Apparent for too many years to be denied the palm. In any event, Butler lost no opportunity to urge upon Churchill the desirability of an earlier rather than a later retirement, in Eden's interests. Here, at any rate, was one period of his career when he could be accused of no ambiguity; nor did he try to back more than one horse.

Macmillan once observed that for a politician to come to the number one post, he must, apart from any abilities or any desirable facets of character he may possess, be lucky. Up to 1955 Butler had been exceptionally lucky. He came into the House just in time to take up his first ministerial post in a department whose affairs meant a great deal to him. He was given, by Churchill, a department the tasks ahead of which he had long considered with care and imagination. He became Chancellor precisely when the country was in a mood for the policies he supported. In 1956 his luck began to go sour, and his indiscretions more dangerous than they had hitherto been. There were many factors, as I have already indicated, in the preference of the party for Macmillan over him in 1957, but probably the one uppermost in most minds early in 1957, when the choice had to be made, was his apparently ambiguous conduct during the Suez affair. And here sheer bad luck got him off on the wrong foot.

At the time of Eden's succession Butler was still borne down by the death, a year earlier, of his first wife, though he was sustained by the friendship, and later the love, of the present Lady Butler, whom he married in 1959. He had also had a gruelling time at the Treasury. In July of 1956 he came down with a virus infection which took weeks rather than days to cure and he was below par for some time after he returned to harness in August. This, unfortunately, was the period of the early moves in the Suez Canal crisis, during which Eden formed his subsequently immovable judgement on the issues at stake and created – through the Suez Committee – an unofficial engine of government which enabled him thereafter to control policy as he wished. Had a completely fit Butler been at his post at that time it is possible that there might have been saner counsels in Cabinet, as there certainly would have been more efficient management. However, some time before this particular crisis in both his own and the nation's affairs, Butler had blotted his copybook with the right – and on the question of Suez.

The issue was this. Eden at the Foreign Office, with the concurrence of the defence departments, and, above all, of the Treasury, had decided to withdraw British troops from the Suez Canal Zone bases and regroup in Cyprus. The Foreign Secretary, at that time extremely sympathetic to Egyptian national aspirations, wished to conclude an agreement with Egypt to that effect. Captain Waterhouse, Major Harry Legge-Bourke, Julian Amery and a number of like-minded members (including, in the early stages, the young Enoch Powell) formed the Suez Group to resist this policy. The group was, in fact, formed in embryo after the military takeover in Egypt in 1952. In 1953 Powell, then still an imperialist, denounced the growing demand for withdrawal as the 'most menacing and insistent demand among Tories ... to get rid of Empire'. At the Margate party conference that year it became perfectly clear – after a rousing reception given to Amery – that feeling in the party against withdrawal was widespread, powerful and far more dangerous than the leadership had hitherto foreseen. Only the authority of Winston Churchill preserved Eden's position. Butler had yet to play his role.

By the end of 1953 the situation was becoming bad enough for Churchill himself to appeal (at the annual lunch of the 1922 Committee on 16 December) for unity to preserve the government's small majority. As the months went by, and in spite of the mounting vociferousness of the rebels, Eden pressed on towards an agreement with Egypt. In truth, the best argument for withdrawal was a purely political one – that a newly nationalist and proudly independent Egypt simply would not go on tolerating the presence of 80,000 British troops in the Zone. The argument of the rebels, on the other hand, was that, whether or not Egypt would tolerate them, the troops had to stay for strategic reasons. And, indeed, after the 1956 fiasco the rebels bitterly pointed out that it was the 1954 withdrawal that had made impossible a speedy and efficient Anglo-French conquest of the Canal itself. However, paramount though the purely political reasons were in his own mind,

Eden, feeling his position in the party weakening, decided to use two tactical devices to get his way. He wheeled Churchill out to back him with his immense prestige, and he brought Butler forward to deploy the economic arguments for withdrawal. Butler, who believed with equal strength in the political and the economic arguments, was perfectly willing.

On 13 July 1954 Eden – who did not attend himself – persuaded Churchill, Butler and Anthony Head, Secretary of State for War, to attend a meeting of the Conservative backbench Services Committee. The meeting was stormy and Butler, who stuck strictly to the economic argument for withdrawal, received the brunt of the criticism. The following day Legge-Bourke resigned the Tory Whip, and the rebels stuck together in subsequent votes. Eden was later to reclaim his position with the right simply by launching the Suez invasion. In any event, he was covered by the mantle of Churchill. Butler was the one who was exposed.

Apart from the fact that Churchill was almost above criticism, it was also widely known that he was going along with the Eden policy of withdrawal only because he was about to retire and hand over to Eden and did not, therefore, think it honourable or proper on his part at this stage to overrule the younger man's plans. Captain Waterhouse made the most of this known divergence of view between Prime Minister and Foreign Secretary in the House of Commons debate on 27 July 1954 about agreement on withdrawal between Britain and Egypt. 'There it is,' he said of the agreement, 'and in this piece of paper we have got all that is left of eighty years of British endeavour, thought and forethought.' At this point, according to Lord Moran, he looked directly down at Churchill, already deeply wounded by a similarly scornful (though from the opposition point of view) attack from Attlee. 'It must be grave for him now,' Waterhouse went on, 'to have to take this decision.'

Churchill intervened late in the debate to deny a charge by Reginald Paget, the Labour MP for Northampton (now Lord Paget, and the only Labour Master of Hounds) that he had covertly encouraged rebellion against Eden. But, in truth, his views on the whole matter were well known. 'I have to say something in the Suez debate,' he had told Moran after the Margate conference, '... I shall put Anthony in front. It's his business. If he likes this policy of scuttle in Egypt he must defend it.' And on 14 July he said: 'It was Anthony's policy, but I had to bear the odium of it. Nobody hates getting out of Egypt more than I do.'

There were, of course, a number of members on the right who, while they deeply regretted leaving Egypt, accepted that there was a serious logic to it; they knew Churchill sympathized with them as well as with the hardliners. Butler was the minister who was exposed and when, in 1957, the question of the succession came up there were many who hesitated, bearing in mind not merely his conduct during the 1956 crisis, but in 1954 as well. And the conclusion was that Rab was still an appeaser.

The question of right and wrong in the Anglo-French invasion of Egypt in collusion with Israel can to this day generate more heat in modern British political discussion than any other subject in modern British history. To a number of Tories – like Edward Boyle and Anthony Nutting, who resigned from the government – it was a crime. It is well to remember, however, that at the very outset of the crisis (which came with Gamal Abdel Nasser's decision to nationalize the Canal in order to raise the funds for the construction of the Aswan Dam which the United States had denied him), practically all national political sentiment, including that of Hugh Gaitskell, who changed his tune only under pressure from his party, was on Eden's side, and sympathetic to his angry and violent reaction to what was undeniably a breach of a solemn and freely entered-into international treaty. What subsequently muddied the waters of controversy, and destroyed Eden, was the extraordinary inefficiency and ham-fistedness of the operation itself, particularly in its political direction, and the many lies told about Anglo-French collusion with Israel. Indeed, the constant lying by ministers in the House of Commons on this subject constitutes one of the most disgraceful episodes in British political history. Even long after Israeli and French sources provided the truth – that the French, the British and the Israelis were in a deliberate conspiracy to unseat Nasser, and that Eden's plea that the Anglo-French force went in only to separate Israel and Egypt was untrue – British ministers, and especially Macmillan in his memoirs, continued to cloud the truth.

It would be impossible to discuss the rights and wrongs of the whole matter here. But it is important to get straight the view that Butler took, first because it was related not to the morality of strong action against Nasser – as Boyle's and Nutting's views were – but to its practicality, and secondly and vitally for a study of Butler's career, because his major and self-destructive indiscretion on the subject demonstrates beyond a doubt that he held throughout exactly the view which Macmillan held only at the very end – that the consequences of Suez for sterling were unbearable, and that scuttle was therefore the only policy. Macmillan gained from this, and Butler lost.

The peculiar tragedy of the Suez crisis was that, from the point of view of relations between Eden and Nasser – and their reaction to one another was central to everything that happened – it began with Eden's dove-like gesture of negotiated withdrawal of British troops from the Canal Zone in 1954. In return for a withdrawal which gratified Egypt's new-found sense of national pride Eden secured Nasser's agreement to maintain the existing structure of the Suez Canal Company – in which the British government owned more than forty per cent of the shares, just as Britain was the largest single user of the Canal itself – and to leave its European management in control, guaranteeing at the same time that the Canal would remain an international waterway, open to shipping of all nations.

The 1954 agreement was unusual as an episode in Egypt's relations with any Western power, being to all appearances amicable. At the same time the NATO powers, led by Britain, were seeking, with the assistance principally of Iraq, to construct a northern tier of alliances against the Soviet Union, in order to bar any move on Russia's part towards the Gulf and the Middle East. To such an alliance Nasser was unalterably opposed, denouncing it as imperialist and neo-colonialist. At the same time, while seeking funds from the United States to construct the Aswan Dam, Nasser had given most of his arms business to Eastern-bloc countries and was, besides, sustaining a guerrilla war against Israel based in the Sinai Desert. Irritated beyond endurance by the Egyptian leader's trafficking with the USSR, the Americans withdrew finance for Aswan and Nassar promptly announced his intention of nationalizing the Canal in order to provide the necessary funds. Britain and France – and particularly Britain – saw themselves as trustees of the Canal for the international community and determined that strong action should immediately be taken: if negotiation and pressure failed, then force should be used. Israel had an entirely different concern – the desire to crush Egyptian bases in Sinai and the Gaza Strip; her opportunities would lie in some sort of alliance with the two Western European powers against Egypt. It should be recorded, however, that trusting neither the French nor the British, and in particular distrusting Selwyn Lloyd, David Ben-Gurion, the Israeli Prime Minister, entered with the greatest reluctance into the alliance. He did so only because of tremendous pressures on him from his Chiefs of Staff to take what seemed a glorious opportunity to strike down Israel's most powerful Arab enemy. In the event all Ben-Gurion's fears, suspicions and hesitations were justified: in spite of overwhelming victories in the Sinai, American pressures eventually forced the Israeli forces to withdraw from the desert, whither they did not return until the war of 1967.

Returning from his illness Butler immediately gave the Prime Minister his full support for the proposition that everything possible should be done to force Nasser to back down. But he was already uneasy – and told his colleagues so – on several grounds. First, he disliked the threat to resort to force. Second, he feared and distrusted Eden's immediate emotional identification of Nasser with Hitler, a tyrant of the same type whose career, if not nipped in the bud, would bring chaos and war to the Middle East. Third, he questioned Eden's and Macmillan's sanguine expectation of full American support, even in an election year. Fourth, he feared the effects on sterling of a major clash in the Middle East. Fifth, he doubted whether Anglo-French forces were up to the kind of fast, surgical operation, rather in the Israeli manner, which could alone be successful before international opprobrium fell on the heads of Britain and France. Sixth and finally he looked with anxiety on the way the Third World, and especially the new Commonwealth powers, were taking sides against the Anglo-French alliance. He observed that Nasser was not at all like Hitler, being the undoubtedly genuine representative of a new nationalism, and not a dictator imposing his will; but he forgot, in saying this, that Hitler was a democratically elected leader – which Nasser was not – and that his popularity, so far as can be judged, was sustained until he began to lose the war. On nearly every point, however, Butler was one hundred per cent correct; he said it all from the beginning, and he was punished for it all at the end.

Most worrying of all for Butler, however, was the extreme

emotional state the Prime Minister had got himself into over the whole matter. The loss of the Canal was accepted by every member of the government as a peculiarly grave matter – much graver than, in fact, it turned out to be. But Eden took the whole thing so desperately, ardently and even violently to heart that his judgement can only be regarded as having been unhinged. Like Macmillan he thought he had objective evidence of American backing: Dulles, the American Secretary of State, had withdrawn the Aswan finance and had denounced Nasser in terms nearly as violent as his own. He did not appreciate, as the cooler Butler did, the fact that Eisenhower, the great soldier, had made his entire pitch to the American people in his first election campaign as the man who would bring peace in Korea, and was utterly determined not to go forward before the electorate in November 1956 (his second election) having sanctioned a war in the Middle East.

Eden found, in succeeding weeks, plenty of good reasons to be bitter and angry towards the United States. It seems, according to the latest evidence, that the various diplomatic moves by which the military operation was delayed were designed by Dulles simply in order to procure postponement – to head off the clash as long as possible. Eden, in all innocence, took them seriously. Thus, there was first a London conference of Canal users. Nasser had planned to attend, but Eden's well-nigh hysterical public language about him made it impossible for him to do so. Then there was a mission to Cairo led by Sir Robert Menzies, the Prime Minister of Australia, but this was undercut by a declaration from Dulles that the United States was eschewing force. The growing conviction around the world that the Americans would not back Britain and France in an invasion also destroyed in its infancy the Suez Canal Users Association, also designed to bring pressure to bear on Egypt. By October the whole scene had darkened, and in his lecture to the Conservative Political Centre at the party conference that month – traditionally one of the high spots of the conference – Butler strove, without being weak, to bring a combined tone of moderation and firmness into the whole debate. After a stout defence of Britain's role in winding up her Empire, and a powerful attack on communism, he said:

> No country in the world has shown more sympathy or given more help to the legitimate aspirations of nationalism, and not least of Arab nationalism, than has ours. But on one point we are adamant: these aspirations can only be achieved in accordance with the rule of law. If international agreements are to be broken and international assets seized with impunity, then world confidence will be shaken irreparably in all territories that rely on outside capital for their development; and the whole policy of the helping hand towards under-developed countries will be gravely and tragically prejudiced. Moreover, there are weightier considerations even than that involved in this issue. For had we abjectly decided to knuckle under to this show of predatory nationalism, what confidence would the under-developed countries have in *us*? What trust could our dependencies and our other friends have placed in our obligations to guide and protect them? What future would we have had then as a great power and a great force for freedom and moral values in the world? The answer is 'None'; for we should have abdicated from our responsibilities and our greatness alike.

This was a powerful and even passionate piece of reasoning, for the purpose of which Butler silenced all his own reservations about what was going on and the way in which policy was being conducted. Reasoned and powerful though it was, however, it was held against him during the subsequent leadership contest as being less fiery than the contemporary utterances of Eden and Macmillan.

Anyway, by now Butler was out of the inner circle planning the Suez invasion. It was almost by accident that he learned from an unhappy Selwyn Lloyd on 18 October that he had been to Paris two days earlier with Eden for a secret conference with Guy Mollet and Antoine Pineau, the French Prime Minister and Foreign Secretary. A secret alliance with Israel was already in the air by which the Israelis would strike at Egypt, and Britain and France would then intervene to separate the combatants and protect the Canal. It was a hare-brained scheme, not because it was militarily faulty but because nobody with a grain of common sense would believe the justification. 'I was impressed', wrote Butler coldly, 'by the audacity of the thinking behind this plan but concerned about the public reaction.' Again, however, as in every major crisis when he disagreed, Butler made no serious protest.

So, on 29 October Israel attacked Egypt. The following day Britain and France sent an ultimatum to both sides to withdraw. The build-up of Allied forces was agonizingly slow. On 4 November there was a rumour that the Israelis had ceased fire, something that would undermine the whole Allied justification. It proved, however, to be untrue. The French and British troops landed and fought their way to within sixty miles of Suez, where they were ordered to stop. The whole secret purpose of the alliance with Israel – to re-take the Canal – was therefore abandoned because Eden found himself trapped with the false and publicly declared argument that his purpose was to separate the two armies. In intention, execution and result the whole business was a shambles.

And this was immediately apparent to most members of Eden's government. Their moment of drastic and even desperate confusion coincided, moreover, with a very serious blunder on Butler's part.

Apart from Eden's reason for stopping the troops there were others, all of them confirming the initial reservations of Butler when he first heard of the plan to use force. The United Nations censured Britain – a more worrying event then than it would be now, especially as most of the Commonwealth ranged themselves against the British move. American speculation against sterling reached danger point, and Harold Macmillan immediately switched sides. Brendan Bracken wrote to Beaverbrook:

> This government is, as you know, in a hell of a mess. Eden's illness is not diplomatic: he is suffering from exhaustion. But it doesn't affect his resolution or his obstinacy.
>
> Until a week ago Macmillan, whose bellicosity was beyond description, was wanting to tear Nasser's scalp off with his own fingernails. He was like that character in O'Casey's play:
>
> Let me like a hero fall,
> My breast expanding to the ball.
>
> Today he might be described as the leader of the bolters. His Treasury officials have put before him the economic consequences of the Suez fiasco and his feet are frost-bitten. You will remember that only ten days ago he declared that the financial cost of the Suez Canal operation will be small. He now finds that it will probably wreck his ... policy ...

Macmillan had the good sense, however, to keep his new views within a very tight circle. Butler was foolish enough to repeat them – as his own, since he agreed with them – at a private dinner with twenty Conservative members of the Progress Trust. 'Wherever I moved', he says, 'in the weeks that followed, I felt the party knives sticking in my back.' At that dinner Macmillan won the leadership.

Just after it, however, Butler again became Acting Prime Minister. Defeat was gall to Eden, and he immediately suffered a serious emotional and physical collapse. It was quite clear, that though his friends and allies – and his doctor – had hopes that he would make a full recovery, he could not for the moment continue in day-to-day charge of the business of government. Yet again Butler was recruited to take charge, while Macmillan waited on the sidelines; it was even Butler, and not the Chancellor, Macmillan, who negotiated the crucial American stand-by finance necessary to rescue sterling. Nor did Eden make things easy for him. It had been decided that the stricken Prime Minister could not find rest anywhere in Britain and he retreated, therefore, to the remote house of the novelist Ian Fleming in Jamaica. He insisted, however, on being kept in touch with events, which could be done only by telegraph to the Governor and subsequent road messenger to the house, 'Goldeneye'. It was indeed, as Butler later said, the most difficult time of his career.

He had to accept willy nilly all the odium attached to the painful business of withdrawal; without immediate compliance with the United Nations resolution on withdrawal American support finance would not be available. This brief period – it lasted until Eden's return on 14 December – was intensely humiliating for nation and government, and what happened then certainly drove the last nails into the coffin of Butler's hopes.

On 8 January Eden telephoned Butler to say that he was on his way to Sandringham to proffer his resignation to the Queen. Lords Kilmuir and Salisbury polled the Cabinet and the parliamentary party before advice was offered to the Sovereign as to whom she should send for. Churchill's recommendation has already been noted. As Butler himself wrote, 'It was clear from the representations that had been made to the Chief Whip's Office that there were many on the backbenches who would oppose my succession; there was no similar anti-Macmillan faction.' And thus Macmillan went to kiss hands; and Butler became Home Secretary.

Denied the premiership, denied even his alternative

dream of the Foreign Office, and barely consoled by being invited to chair the Cabinet on Macmillan's frequent foreign trips, Butler was at least given a free hand at the Home Office, notoriously, because it has become the dustbin into which so many unwanted responsibilities are dumped, one of the most intractable departments in Whitehall. He records that Macmillan regarded the many reforms he undertook there 'in a similar spirit of indulgent scepticism, it seemed, as Churchill had shown fifteen years earlier towards my work for education'. Nevertheless, unwearied and unbowed, Butler again set his hand to the plough, and beyond an increasingly ironical and cynical mode of private utterance, showed nothing in the way of bitterness or resentment at his being passed over.

Macmillan has said that on becoming Prime Minister he did not immediately form his Private Office. In particular, he did not invite his old and loyal friend John Wyndham (later Lord Egremont) to join him, because he did not expect his government to last very long. In the event, he performed a miracle of political reconstruction, though at an economic cost that is still being paid.

His manner, and the exceptionally disciplined skill of his Chief Whip, Edward Heath, served quickly to restore the unity, and to some extent the morale, of the party. He determined immediately to reflate the economy, so as to produce a pre-election boom. A year later, all three of his Treasury Ministers (Peter Thorneycroft, Nigel Birch and Enoch Powell) resigned in protest against what they considered to be profligate and dangerously inflationary policies. Macmillan dismissed the matter, and sailed blithely on, earning his reputation for unflappability, to a triumphant election victory in 1959. Almost immediately, however, things began to go wrong for him, not least because of a sharp downturn in the economy, which he had helped to create by his post-1957 policies. After a short interval he replaced Thorneycroft at the Treasury with Selwyn Lloyd, but Butler never achieved, under Macmillan, his ambition of the Foreign Office, that post going to Lord Home.

Butler was now out of the real centre of things. He still had multifarious responsibilities, and they were even to increase. He remained Leader of the House and Chairman of the party until 1961, when Iain Macleod replaced him, and he lost the Home Office – becoming Deputy Prime Minister – in July 1962, in the panic of the 'night of long knives' when a desperate Macmillan, his government floundering in deeper and deeper water every day, carried out the most drastic Cabinet reconstruction of modern times.

Butler set himself to bring order to the Home Office, applying the same progressive and liberal instincts that had sustained him all those years ago at the Department of Education and his own special brand of emollient tact and quiet efficiency to the task of administering the place. To this day he is particularly proud of his record as Home Secretary, and that pride is justified if only in the fact that he did himself no serious damage there, for the Home Office has been the graveyard of many political reputations. Very early on he nearly became the victim of a bugging scandal – the police were eavesdropping on conversations between a barrister and a well-known criminal – and after he had defused the matter he began to take to going into the House of Commons smoking room each evening in order to pick up any hint of difficulty or scandal that might embarrass him or his department.

In spite of the remark by Moran which I quoted earlier, to the effect that Butler is not socially an easy man, I have always found him convivial, if a little strange. It is odd, therefore, that a politician of his ambition had on no occasion in his long career made a haunt of the smoking room, always a favourite resort of Churchill's, and somewhere Harold Macmillan could always be found during leadership crises. It is certainly true that Butler found his evenings there – even his useful evenings – tiresome: the company was not up to his preferred standard. But it is strange all the same that even minimal effort was beyond him in his pursuit of the top job.

For all his pride in his Home Office record it can hardly be said that what Butler did there was of major importance. What he managed to do was convey the impression of the liberal-minded Home Secretary *par excellence*. One of his principal problems was his inheritance of a Homicide Act which distinguished between different kinds of punishment for different kinds of murder, the intention being to employ the death penalty only where the death penalty might reasonably be thought to deter. Although on entering his new department Butler had no more than a vague predisposition against capital punishment he left in 1962 a resolute opponent of it. Uncharacteristically, this new conviction did not arise out of long or settled thought, but from his experience of being, in effect, the last court of appeal for the life of a condemned prisoner, it then being the Home Secretary's duty to decide whether or not to recommend reprieve. It took him, he recalls, at least two days to make such decisions, and according to his friends it took a lot longer to recover from having made one.

Butler put through a good deal of miscellaneous, but invariably contentious legislation at the Home Office. He saw through laws on prostitution (to clear the streets of London of soliciting girls), on charities, and on immigration. The first and last of these caused him a good deal of pain. In the matter of the prostitutes trouble arose because he was a vice-president of the Association for Moral and Social Hygiene, which had been founded in 1870 by a member of his family, Josephine Butler. The Association objected to the Bill because, while it greatly increased the penalties imposed on the girls it did little to inflict punishment on men, especially the pimps. Butler argued that his Bill did contain such provision, but that the police had convinced him that, whereas it was relatively easy to find and convict the girls, it was much harder to do the same to the men. The Association was not convinced, and he was compelled to resign as vice-president.

The immigration legislation tarnished his liberal image. It was the first Act in the British Parliament to deny the total applicability of the view implied in the sentence *Civis Britannicus sum* to natives of the Commonwealth. While Butler defended it on the impeccably logical principle that the increasing and uncontrolled numbers of Commonwealth citizens coming into Britain would make good race relations far more difficult, his Bill none the less raised an enormous furore. The Labour Party solemnly undertook to repeal it upon taking office: when the time came to draft their 1964 manifesto, however, they had decided to promise to keep it and, indeed, they subsequently introduced far less justifiable immigration control legislation. It seems to me that one of the few things in his past that Butler remains personally bitter about is the criticism he had to endure during the passage of the Immigration Bill.

In March 1962 Macmillan sent for Butler. He had yet another new task to proffer, one which Butler was to hold, in addition to all his other responsibilities, until July of that year. Macmillan recalled, and emphasized, that during the war his career had been made by being 'put on a limb' as Minister Resident in North Africa. He wanted Butler to take a similar risk by taking charge, as Secretary of State, of the affairs of the Central African Federation, consisting of what are now the three independent countries of Malawi, Zambia and Zimbabwe. What Butler would have to recommend, he knew from the start, would be either a break-up of the Federation, beginning with the secession of Malawi (then Nyasaland), or some modification of its existing structure. To procure either he would have to overcome the formidable opposition not only of the

Rhodesian whites, but of the powerful Federal Prime Minister, Sir Roy Welensky. To procure any compromise he would have to overcome perhaps what was in the long run the even more formidable opposition of Hastings Banda, the Nyasaland leader, and Kenneth Kaunda, the rapidly emerging chief of the Northern Rhodesian (Zambian) nationalists. He did the job in a matter of months, and there has seldom been a piece of diplomacy carried out with such skill and deftness.

It was Butler's anxious wish – and in this he was supported by Home, whom he consulted before accepting the job – to preserve something of the Federation if he possibly could. He did not altogether agree with his advisers (one of whom was Lord Alport, a former Governor of Kenya, but also a former Conservative Research Department associate of post-war days) that the secession of Nyasaland at least had to be immediately accepted, and he bent his powers of persuasion to make Dr Banda go slowly. The difficulty he was in was that whereas there could be no question of taking the powers of government away from the Southern Rhodesian whites – a large, powerful and determined minority, as their subsequent history has shown – there could be no prospect of preserving in Nyasaland or Northern Rhodesia any regime or federation unacceptable to Banda and Kaunda. At last, Butler was forced to bow to the inevitable, and the Federation came to an end.

Although a vital interlude in the history of the last days of the British Empire this was nevertheless a brief one, in history and in Butler's career. But it was of considerable interest, and remains of interest to the student of Butler's life, for the effect it had on his reputation, both at home and abroad.

The extent to which Butler retained to the end the confidence of white and black leaders alike was remarkable. Even in his splenetically polemical volume of memoirs, *4,000 Days*, Sir Roy Welensky, who excoriates both

Macmillan and the Colonial Secretary, Iain Macleod (who was, by contrast, loved by the blacks and was godfather to Hastings Banda's son), professes his respect and regard for Butler. And while during the final negotiations Welensky would not allow his people and the Central African Office civil servants to dine together, he took care to be punctilious in his courtesy to the Butlers. Where Butler's skill was shown, and where he won the respect of all, was in the way he did not prevaricate or, like Macleod or Macmillan, speak to any of his interlocutors in ambiguous terms, unusual though that judgement may be of him. It was a gentle process, one of bringing other men – and other kinds of men – around to belief in his own view of what was inevitable. It was an exercise which, however complicated and fraught with danger (there was a moment when Welensky threatened to send troops into Northern Rhodesia following a disturbance), was none the less narrow in scope and in time. But even allowing for its limitations, and for the powerful forces that were pressing along towards the dissolution of the Federation, Butler's achievement was remarkable.

When Butler had just about finished his task, at the Victoria Falls conference, the *Rhodesia Herald* wrote:

> A month ago the Falls Conference was regarded as impossible. First with Mr Field [the Prime Minister of Southern Rhodesia] then with the Northern Rhodesian leaders, and finally with a highly suspicious and sensitive Sir Roy Welensky, Mr Butler has exercised his extraordinary charm and logic to produce this result within an hour of the conference opening ...The subtle moulding influence of Mr Butler appeared to show itself again because the five speakers who followed him all followed broadly the same line in spite of their varied standpoints.

It was, indeed, a performance that had a touch of magic

about it.

The end of the story of the Federation came, of course, only in 1980, with the independence of Zimbabwe; and it came only after a long and bloody war. During the course of the negotiations that began, in effect, with the Commonwealth Prime Ministers' Conference in Lusaka in 1979 I had the opportunity to question Dr Kaunda, Dr Banda and Sir Roy about their memories of the history and final break-up of the Federation. Sir Roy held strictly to the line of his memoirs, that is, he was sharply critical of British policy in general, and remained bitter about Macleod and Macmillan especially. For Butler he evinced a warm, if slightly wary, personal regard. The two black leaders, as might be expected, waxed lyrical in their enthusiasm for Macleod: he was, after all, their partisan. But what struck me as exceptional, given both the length of time that had elapsed and the brevity of his involvement in their affairs, was the regard and respect that they still had for Butler, and the freshness of their memory of his negotiating technique. My first discussion on the matter with President Kaunda came before the Lusaka conference opened, and he was apprehensive about how things would go, as well as suspicious of the intentions of Mrs Thatcher in regard to the government of Bishop Abel Muzorewa, then ruling in Salisbury. My first inquiry about his memory of Butler was a casual one, but it elicited not merely a paean of praise, but an outburst of nostalgia, to the effect that if only Butler had been coming to Lusaka all might be well.

There are those in British politics today who would say that praise from Kenneth Kaunda most certainly, in their eyes, damns the record and policies of R.A.Butler. Certainly, the support and plaudits he managed to elicit for himself in Africa in 1962 and 1963 were not echoed in crucial Tory circles at home, where he was felt to have betrayed a great cause, that of the white man and his legacy in Africa.

Butler was thus irredeemably fixed with a record of softness over Suez and weakness in the face of challenge in Central Africa. And his last leadership crisis was fast approaching.

Central Africa was also Butler's last great challenge, for his brief year in the Foreign Office during Home's premiership could, in the nature of things, and with a general election looming over the government, hardly produce much of substance. It was merely a formal gratification of a long-held wish, and while he set about his task there with his customary diligence he had neither time nor opportunity for achievement. Of what he did in Africa, however, while there may be differing views about the choice of course, there can be none about the skill with which he handled an exceptionally difficult and potentially explosive situation. Moreover, just as this was a new arena for him, so he displayed in action in it new qualities, or at least qualities that had not always been all that much in evidence before. I have said that his whole negotiating posture was a conciliatory one, and that he leant very much on the diplomatic arts to procure the support of men so diverse in their natures and objects as Kaunda, Welensky, and Banda. But at the Victoria Falls conference, which he chaired, he also showed steel, interpreting the rules of the conference in quite a narrow way, ruling all diversions ruthlessly out of order and forcing his strong-willed and often temperamental participants into a procedural mould entirely of his own making. All this he got away with, and if subsequent relations between the participating parties – even between Banda and Kaunda – were never very good, he had none the less averted what could have been an exceptionally nasty and bloody war in which Britain, because of the depth of her involvement in Central Africa at that time would necessarily have become embroiled, just as the Belgians were embroiled in the Congo.

Butler confesses that he was excited at the initial prospect of the African job. Truth to tell, he may have been finding the Home Office somewhat dull. But his acceptance of this, as it turned out, final challenge, and chance to play imperial proconsul at last had, I believe, little to do with taking on an adventure, for all that his pulse quickened. It was rather of a piece with his whole career – the willing acceptance of whatever public task was laid upon him, however disagreeable or dangerous to his career it might turn out to be.

7
The Last Act

Such are Macmillan's beguiling skills as a political actor-manager that it is easy to forget for how brief a time during his six years and nine months as Prime Minister did he enjoy that untroubled ascendancy in the country with which tradition now credits him. He inherited, of course, a virtually impossible situation, his predecessor driven out of office, a failure so great having taken place that it was widely felt that Britain was finished as an international power, a party riven by discord, and a nation plunged into the depths of gloom. He proceeded to resolve that situation within months and lead that divided party to a spectacular triumph at the polls over a baffled and shell-shocked opposition less than three years later. But less than two years after that famous victory Britain was plunged into economic depression, further humiliated by General de Gaulle's veto on her entry into the European Economic Communities, Macmillan was without a policy, and both his nerve and health were failing. Moreover – and this was a particularly sore point for a man so committed to his standards of personal probity – the government was shaken again and again by scandal, first by espionage in the Civil Service (the Vassall affair) and then by the behaviour of a minister, John Profumo, both in engaging in an affair with a lady of easy virtue and then lying to his colleagues and the House of Commons about it.

In July 1962, therefore, in the face of all these blows, Macmillan decided on that radical reconstruction of his government to which reference has already been made. Butler did not suffer from this, at least in dignity: he lost the Home Office, but retained Central Africa and was formally designated First Secretary of State and Deputy Prime Minister. Macmillan has since said that he feels he should have undertaken this reconstruction shortly after the 1959 general election; it was designed, after all, to bring forward new and younger men, and to give the government and the party a complete facelift. It achieved that end and created, as Butler observes, one of the strongest of post-war Cabinets. But the timing was all wrong: had it been done in the fresh period after the general election it would have won unstinting praise, but when done under the pressure of events – many of them sordid – it was judged redolent of panic. And the dismissal of the ever-loyal Selwyn Lloyd, not just from the Treasury, but altogether from the government, smacked of cruelty and disloyalty as well as panic. During the brief period remaining to him Macmillan never regained his reputation for *sang-froid*: that had to wait for his emergence in retirement as a television personality.

During this period Butler reflected a great deal on the way things were going. On his return from Africa he wrote for his private use a memorandum on the general situation. It said, *inter alia*:

> ...my diagnosis shows that there is a very strong movement in favour of somebody for the leadership not too

> closely associated with the Establishment. What is really happening in the party is that the herd instinct is unleashed and that they are tending to attack anybody in authority starting with the Prime Minister, including the Chief Whip, Martin Redmayne, and also embracing the leaders of the 1922 Committee, who are thought to be too old world. These in their turn are not making much stand against the herd and are tending to accept the drift. There is not so much positive approval of a younger man as there is a recognition that this may make a clearer picture for the next election... That they do so was confirmed to me in a talk by the Chief Whip who said there was a move to make a caretaker government under me but that strong preference was to go for the next generation.

And he concluded:

> When I talked to the P.M. he was not in a happy mood and was resigned to the fact that he would probably have to go. His own preference was for waiting some time, perhaps even until the party conference. His anxiety, he said, was to retain the discretion of the Crown so that the Crown could choose whomever she wished. There is a considerable discussion going on as to the method of choosing a leader. If there is clearly a big majority for one candidate then I think the rest of us should pull in and help. I think a leader of the Conservative party, as Pretyman said in 1921, should *emerge* and that this is the only lasting way of achieving a result.

So, Butler was girding his loins for his final effort.

At this stage, as Butler says, Macmillan was actively contemplating an early departure, though that was not something he very much wanted to do. However, he had never been insensible to the necessity of making some provision for the succession; and he was acutely aware of the general belief that, in staying as long as he did,

Churchill had damaged the national interest. On the other hand, Macmillan was influenced by several different considerations. If he had to go before the next general election (to be held, at the latest, in October 1964) he felt, like Churchill, that he should leave the new man neither too little time to play himself in, nor so much time that he would be saddled by the blunders and unpopularity of Macmillan's own administration. He also considered that it might be best for the party if he soldiered on to an election defeat – supposing such to be inevitable – thus leaving his successor a clean slate. (In the same fashion Butler thought it might be unwise to saddle one of the next generation with a defeat, since his future might thereby be damaged; better by far, was Butler's thought, for an older man to lose, if lose the Tories must.) Finally, Macmillan was determined to have a major say in the succession: as it is easy to show from the more honest memoirs of the contest for the leadership, and particularly from the reminiscences of Macleod and Powell, Macmillan deliberately, and by misrepresenting the evidence before him, left the Queen little choice as to whom to send for. His remarks to Butler about preserving the royal prerogative were a smokescreen.

In considering the succession, and especially after the 'night of the long knives', Macmillan, dead set against Butler, had three candidates in mind: Hailsham, the Leader of the House of Lords (Macmillan having passed legislation enabling a member of the Upper House to disclaim his peerage), Maudling, now Chancellor of the Exchequer, and Macleod, Chairman of the party and Leader of the House of Commons. For Hailsham and Macleod it could be said that they were both outstanding orators, and perhaps just the type to rally the party in the face of the adversity that threatened to overwhelm it. Against Hailsham was his suspect judgement and his tendency to temperament; but Hailsham had Oliver Poole, the co-Chairman of the party and its senior *éminence grise*, rooting for him. Against Macleod was the suspicion the right felt towards him for his liberal record in Africa and a similar suspicion that he was calculating and devious – like Butler in fact. For Maudling was the fact that the appeared to be handling the Treasury with brilliance and aplomb, this being before the devastating attacks on his record launched by Harold Wilson during the Home premiership. Against him was his reputation of being easy-going, lazy and too fond of the good things of life. But Macmillan gave each of these men in turn a good run to show their paces. To Butler he showed no favour.

For all that there was strong feeling that the time for a change was nigh, there were many who believed that Macmillan should stay and, indeed, that of all the contenders he was the one most likely to stage a recovery and bring off the Tories' fourth successive election victory; Macleod was the most prominent politician in this camp. As autumn arrived and the party conference approached it was becoming clear to Macmillan that none of his three horses had emerged with an indisputable lead, though he still had a strong hankering after Hailsham. On 11 September Butler dined with the Prime Minister at Chequers and subsequently wrote to Home:

> His state of mind is as follows: his aim for us is either to defeat the Socialists at the next election or so to achieve an election result that they have no overwhelming majority and can be turned out within the space of one Parliament...
>
> He has by no means made up his mind. I noticed the same hankering as I have seen in P.M.'s minds before, especially Churchill before retirement, to stay in office and achieve something lasting. We know how difficult this is ... I said it would be tragic if after seven successful years there should be a big break with the

> party in the House. He himself realises that it would be a thankless task to remain P.M., fight an election, perhaps lose and then have to submit to change. He expressed some doubt whether he was in the mood for another election.

By now Westminster was discussing virtually no other subject than the future leadership of the Conservative Party. The Chief Whip felt that, if pressed, he could arrange a rallying around Butler, but he was clearly by no means enthusiastic.

Meanwhile, Macmillan's mood was hardening. On 7 October he told Butler that he did not want to make a final announcement at the party conference the following Saturday (at this time, and until the election of Edward Heath, Conservative leaders did not attend the conference until the last day, when they addressed the final rally). However, at the morning Cabinet the following day, 8 October, Macmillan was taken ill. By the afternoon it was clear that his health (he had an enlarged prostate gland) would not allow him to contest an election. A new choice would have to be made, and it would be much influenced by the fevered atmosphere of the Blackpool conference. As was now becoming usual, Butler took on the role of Acting Prime Minister.

A great deal has been written about the events that followed, and nearly every participant has set down his views. The most pungently expressed are those of Iain Macleod and Enoch Powell ('How Macmillan lied to the Queen') in the *Spectator*. But it is fair to say that the general opinion nowadays is that Macmillan rigged the results of the supposedly exhaustive investigations into whom the party wanted as his successor (conducted by Lords Dilhorne, St Aldwyn and Poole, Mr John Morrison and the Chief Whip in the Commons) which he incorporated in his report to the Queen. Throughout the contest Butler behaved with a slightly limp-wristed dignity. He received deputations. He was available at all times to his supporters. But he could not manage to make a stirring speech at the Blackpool conference, where, after a certain amount of dissension, he was allowed to stand in for Macmillan – and he refused to intrigue. All along he told those who asked him that he would serve under anybody who convinced him he could unite the party.

Blackpool was a bear garden. Home brought Macmillan's announcement, that he could not go on, from London and, in his capacity as Chairman of the National Union, and thus Chairman for Butler's speech at the final rally, read it to an audience in tumult. One of the problems of having the opening stages of the leadership contest staged at the party conference was that it provided the public spectacle of a party tearing itself to pieces. Another was the simple fact that the favourite contenders of the party in the country were by no means the same as the favourite contenders of the party in Parliament. Thus, Blackpool was the stage from which Hailsham announced his decision to disclaim his peerage, and Blackpool was the place where, because of a fine speech and his assertion of a chairman's firm authority when Butler met some heckling during the rally, Home first emerged in the public eye (and the eye of the press) as a potential dark horse candidate. But both Home and Hailsham were already vastly popular with the party rank and file; it was hardly surprising that in the rather wild atmosphere of the conference town the yearning of the delegates to have a real say in the decision should come to the fore. Nevertheless, Hailsham's extravagant behaviour at Blackpool confirmed to most of those who could most readily influence the decision – members of the Cabinet and of the House of Commons – that he would not do.

Butler, by contrast, had a lack-lustre conference. He was humiliated, first, by being subjected to a lengthy discussion by his colleagues on whether or not the Saturday rally should be cancelled, whether Butler should merely read out the speech Macmillan had prepared, or whether he should be allowed to make a speech of his own. The third of these options having been decided upon, Butler made a speech restating his own philosophy of Toryism, but one which, though it reads exceptionally well, and is a most cogent piece of work, went down badly as a piece of oratory. There was also, in its course, that vivid moment to which I have already referred when Home rose to insist on silence for the Acting Prime Minister. He was greeted by ecstatic applause, and the contrast with the reception accorded his colleague was lost neither on the press nor on the public watching television.

In any event, Macmillan had already added Home's name to the list of contenders and at or around this time Home agreed to stand, but only if it was clear that he was going to win: he would accept the job only if he were the favourite on the poll, not if he had to fight for it. Indeed later on, when he had begun to realize how many of his Cabinet colleagues were against him, he suspected Macmillan of playing around somewhat with the figures, for he telephoned the Prime Minister to say that he had thought he was coming to heal, not to wound. To this Macmillan replied with the, as Macleod puts it, 'curious observation' that '...we can't change our views now. All the troops are on the starting line. Everything is arranged ...'

Though it was possible for business to go forward in greater peace – or secrecy – in London than in Blackpool, the temperature of events remained at fever pitch in the week after the conference. The key day, as Macleod calls it, was 17 October. By then Macmillan was ready with all his material; not surprisingly, the Tories in the House of Lords were heavily in favour of their fellow-peer. More surprisingly, it was claimed that Home had a slight majority in the Commons. Most surprisingly it was also claimed that he had a majority in the Cabinet. It is on this last claim that the argument about Macmillan's conduct principally turns, for, as Macleod observed, the manner in which the poll of MPs was conducted, with the Chief Whip and others pressing hard for Home, made all sorts of interpretation of the result possible, especially given that the Whips were exercising a somewhat arcane system of proportional representation of their own for which, of course, there was no constitutional authority whatsoever.

In the course of the morning Macleod consulted Maudling about a rumour that the succession was to be decided that afternoon. As he later observed:

> It is some measure of the tightness of the magic circle on this occasion that neither the Chancellor of the Exchequer nor the Leader of the House of Commons (and, he might have added, Chairman of the party) had any inkling of what was going to happen.

In the course of the day Macleod, Maudling and Powell put their heads together. Powell and Macleod both spoke to Home on the telephone and gave him their view that he was not the right choice, Macleod having a particular right to address him in this way because of the two jobs he held. That evening Powell, Macleod, Maudling, Frederick Erroll and, later, the Chief Whip, met at Powell's house in South Eaton Place. They were joined at various times by other ministers and they were in constant touch by telephone with Hailsham.

It became clear that, besides Powell and Macleod, who were the strongest supporters of Butler, being determined not to serve under anybody else, both Maudling and Hailsham who were still, though vestigially, contenders, were for Butler over Home. All through this period it is a striking fact that Macmillan kept every string in his own hands as he lay in bed in the King Edward VII Hospital for Officers. He declined to allow a meeting of the Cabinet to take place, and frequently declined to accept or return telephone calls from colleagues. He must have been acutely aware of the risks he was running: had he allowed the Cabinet to come together it would have speedily become apparent that the majority for Home which he wished to pretend existed did not, in fact, have any life outside his own imagination.

This can be demonstrated from indisputable facts in the accounts of events given by Macleod and Powell. According to Randolph Churchill's *The Fight for the Tory Leadership*, the single narrative, apart from his own memoirs, which supports Macmillan, Dilhorne arrived at Macmillan's hospital bed on the morning of the 17th and reported that most of the Cabinet were for Home. Now, on the 18th, five members of the Cabinet met for lunch; their number did not include Butler himself, Hailsham or Sir Edward Boyle. Not one was for Home, and the three absentees I have mentioned were all, of course, for Butler. Macleod and Powell both assert (and nobody other than the Macmillan and Home partisans has ever seriously disputed their view) that at least eleven members of the Cabinet were definitely against Home, and only two for. That left half a dozen members: in the unlikely event of none of these being for either Butler or Hailsham it would still be impossible to argue, as Macmillan says he did in his memorandum to the Queen, that the overwhelming majority of the Cabinet was for Home. In the event Home was so far from believing the account Macmillan gave the Queen that when she invited him to form a government he declined to kiss hands – the act of a Prime Minister on assuming the post – and instead merely undertook to attempt to do so.

On the evening of the meeting at Powell's house several of those present (including Hailsham) telephoned Butler at St Ermin's Hotel, where he and his wife were staying while repairs to their house in Smith Square were being effected. All these calls were calls of sympathy and support. Mrs Butler, combative like Powell and Macleod, advised, even begged, her husband to refuse to serve. Other members of the Cabinet – and the mounting list of names makes the Macmillan thesis of overwhelming support for Home even more preposterous – including Boyle, John Boyd-Carpenter and Butler's successor at the Home Office, Henry Brooke, telephoned with offers of support.

The following morning, after a formal meeting of ministers, Butler telephoned Dilhorne. He asked the Lord Chancellor to arrange a meeting of the candidates opposed to Home – Hailsham, Maudling and himself – so that Macmillan would know how strong the opposition to his favourite was. Dilhorne attempted to do this, but Macmillan declined to take his call. A little later Maudling and Hailsham visited Butler to repeat their willingness to follow his lead. But by then Home was at the Palace.

Immediately after lunch Home sent for Butler and told him that unless he and Maudling were willing to serve he could not go on. In the evening Home, Butler, Hailsham and Maudling met together, accompanied by the Chief Whip. It became apparent that Hailsham and Maudling were taking a softer line than Macleod and Powell: they preferred Butler, but were willing to serve under Home. Butler asked for the night to think things over. By the morning he had agreed to serve. As Dilhorne wrote to him on 23 October:

> By your action you have held together the Tory party at a very critical time. I do not doubt that if you had refused to serve, Alec would have failed to form a government and if you had then been sent for, which seems most likely, I think you would have started under very heavy criticism, for it would indeed be hard to justify a refusal to serve on a ground of policy – for there was no difference of policy – and differences of policy are really the only justification for refusing to serve a colleague. Many would have thought that you had refused to serve

> Alec only to secure your personal advantage and that would certainly have done serious harm to your standing. As it is your reputation stands tremendously high for the way in which you behaved in a situation of the very greatest personal difficulty.

At about the same time Martin Redmayne told Butler that it would have been possible to alter the decision in his favour, but that he would never thereafter have been happy. 'With this diagnosis', Butler wrote, 'I agree.'

I have made clear my judgement that Macmillan engaged in a conspiracy to prevent Butler succeeding him. But it is not enough simply and baldly to contrast the Prime Minister's behaviour with Butler's own self-sacrificing, public-spirited and loyal conduct. Enoch Powell, who has a much more ruthless, blood-and-thunder approach to politics, felt something very near contempt for Butler's refusal to strike Home down – as Home himself admitted he could have done. But the matter cannot be confined to the No. 10 meetings that took place after Home had been to the Palace: it all started much earlier.

Writing of the 1957 succession Butler observes that whereas he, borne down by the burden of government, had not time to organize his supporters, Macmillan had his well-organized and marching in advance. Whatever the facts about 1957 it is indisputable that, in 1963, Butler did nothing to organize his troops until it was far, far too late. It is perfectly possible reasonably to argue that Butler was not faced simply with a choice between serving or bringing down the roof on Home's head. Had he begun to put a team together from the moment he knew Macmillan could not continue, the situation would, by 17–18 October, have been far clearer. He could, for example, when he visited Macmillan in hospital before going north to Blackpool, have made it known that he intended to fight a battle; that he did not seems merely to have confirmed Macmillan in his long-standing opinion that Butler simply had not got the meat of the matter in him.

Again, at Blackpool, Butler was almost supine. In the dispute over who should deliver the speech to the rally he left his colleagues to debate the matter by themselves: there was no insistence on his part. He spoke to anybody who wanted to speak to him, affirmed that he very much wanted to be Prime Minister, and admitted that he thought himself by far the best qualified candidate. But he did not try to urge people on. If Hailsham's candidacy was mounted with an extravagance and a vehemence that proved ultimately destructive, it could equally be argued that Butler lost the job by inanition.

Even when the conference had ended and all concerned had returned to London it was clear that Mrs Butler – loyal, devoted and possessed of a personality both attractive and determined – was stronger in her husband's cause than he was himself. Butler merely went the rounds of his daily duties, saw his friends, listened, slumped to the gossip, watched the steady emergence of Alec Home, surmised accurately that Macmillan was engaged on a masterly and ruthless intrigue – and did nothing. In the circumstances it was little short of astonishing and a great tribute to his fundamental power of personality and the excellence of his record that men of naturally passionate and committed natures, particularly Powell and Macleod, stood by his standard to the bitter end, and even refused to follow his surrender. It is almost as though he had a fatalistic conviction that the thing would never go his way, whatever he did.

Once one looks at Butler in this perspective – not simply as the man who refused to make a last-ditch stand against his rival, but a man who, all along, did so little to help himself – one must admit that the question of the validity of Macmillan's analysis of his character must arise again. Was, or is there, something in Butler's nature that made him, for all his great gifts, unfitted for the highest post, unable to find within himself the resolution and the steel (Macmillan's word) required for the efficient discharge of the highest responsibility? Would this man have had the strength – he certainly had the vision – to rally a battered party and lead it to victory at the polls? Could he, thereafter, have governed with the ruthlessness that Britain's declining economic and industrial situation required – a task at which the far younger and more energetic Harold Wilson failed so dismally?

It is impossible, of course, to be certain about any of these things. Home, after all, who had many things against him, who was a wretched performer on television, and who ran a very flickering campaign, came within an ace of victory; it is impossible to say whether the innate decency and straightforwardness of his nature got through to the electorate, or whether there was a last-minute scamper away from Harold Wilson's socialism. In my opinion Butler could have done at least as well; and he also had the priceless advantage, as Macleod observed, of having a proven appeal to voters who were not Conservative, which Home did not possess.

Could he have governed effectively? There is nothing in his record, save his lack-lustre approach to contests for the leadership, which suggests that he could not, and he had, as Macleod again observed, a remarkable capacity for doing better in any job than he was expected to. There is no doubt that he discharged his duties as stand-in for both Eden and Churchill in 1953 most effectively; his two subsequent periods as Acting Prime Minister were too brief to enable any serious judgement to be formed on his capacity. But there are certain indications in his career – notably his handling of the Victoria Falls conference – which suggest that once indisputably in charge he could behave with power and decision.

Anthony Howard, who has been selected as Butler's official biographer, has chosen as his title *The Uncrowned*

Prime Minister. It is a most apt title, though it (like much of the present book) has implications that could easily be judged unfair to Butler. After all, the man has had an extraordinary career of brilliant public service, and even if he is judged to have been found badly wanting either before the Second World War or during the Suez crisis, the depth of the distinction with which he served the state (and his party) can hardly be doubted by any serious critic or historian. The same question does always arise, however: why did he not become Prime Minister? Was it circumstances? Was it the plotting of Macmillan? Was it some fatal flaw in the man himself? And the answer, as usual in these cases, is probably something of all three.

And there is one other factor which has cropped up again and again in the course of these pages. It is that, despite his loyalty amounting almost to servitude to his party, in spite of his repeatedly eschewing ambition, in spite of his lack of ruthlessness in pursuit of personal ends, in spite of the fact that he has a legion of devoted admirers, in spite of all these and many other things, Butler has always managed to raise doubt, suspicion and dislike wherever he has gone. This is not merely a matter of criticism of him for, say, his stand on appeasement, or for his apparent disloyalty during the Suez operation. It is not, in a word, a criticism of his supposed weakness, or his supposed unsoundness on policy matters. It is, rather, a profound suspicion of something in the man that his enemies (and even his milder critics) seem not altogether able to define. Of course many have resented (and have had cause to resent) the sharpness of his tongue, or his undoubted intellectual arrogance, his apparent detachment from ordinary concerns, his lofty air, his occasional verbal cruelty, his many indiscretions, smoothed over and blotted out in his book. But even the sum of all these things does not convey the total effect which, again and again, has ensured a solid body of backbench Conservative opinion opposed to Butler, and not all of them by any means on the right of the party.

As Iain Macleod said, it was a great failing of Butler's that he liked to be a politician among dons and a don among politicians, playing the aloof, objective and dispassionately amused scholar when his political colleagues were thrashing about in the midst of some dreadful crisis, and playing the worldly wise, cynical, earthy man of the outside world among his academic colleagues at Trinity. As usual, there is some real perception in Macleod's remark. Butler is an inveterate role player: one always feels he has some conception of himself, some view about how R.A. Butler ought to do things and how he ought to behave, which he deliberately and bafflingly keeps hidden from anyone who is with him.

There is no possible ground for questioning his absolute commitment to an ideal of public service: that commitment was and is held to a degree and with a fervour more usually found in men and women greatly his inferiors in intelligence. It is exceptional in a man with his kind of philosophical and sceptical, as well as speculative, mind. But at every turn in his career service of the public – or the party – has been put before his own instinct or his own ambition.

It is interesting to speculate on what would have happened to Butler and Home had Home managed to win the 1964 election. The conventional opinion (which I share) is that the Labour Party would then have split asunder and the Conservatives would have been faced with the exceptional challenge of re-making themselves in government as they once did in opposition, after 1945. It is unlikely that Butler would have been a creative Foreign Secretary, in the sense of one striking out in new directions, for formulating new policies: for all his ability at technical diplomacy he never showed himself innovative in foreign affairs. Besides, he would have had behind him a Prime Minister of exceptionally strong character and views whose entire senior experience was in foreign policy. In my view they would have made a remarkable combination.

It is also important to remember that Butler remained as Chairman of the party's Advisory Committee on Policy until the defeat of 1964. Furthermore, when Home appointed Edward Du Cann as Chairman of the party, Du Cann's brief was to embark on a programme of ruthless reform. Home never had the time as Prime Minister to show what he could do, as Butler never had the time as Foreign Secretary. For all their differences, they had striking similarities, particularly in their single-minded devotion to service, shown as much by Home in his career after 1964 as it was by Butler in his earlier years.

Yet in the event, retirement and Trinity were what came his way. And whatever the answer to all the imponderable questions just raised, there remains a feeling that, for all his achievements, this man – in the words of Iain Macleod, 'mystifying, complex and hard to approach...' – was never fully stretched.

8
The Heritage of an English Life

I mentioned in Chapter 1, in the course of describing the excellent relations Butler enjoyed with the staff of the Conservative Research Department, how he particularly ingratiated himself with the department's Establishment Officer, Miss Avis Lewis, by establishing first-class relations with her bull mastiffs. According to her the first thing he used to do on entering her room was to offer the dog his hand, something many of her visitors would, quite simply, be too scared to do. When I retailed that to a hostile critic of Butler's – a man who had worked with him for many years – he observed: 'I bet he offered the brute the crippled hand.'

That little anecdote illustrates nicely the ambivalence and ambiguity of judgement on Butler which has been the recurring theme of this study. It is not merely that what Butler has said and done himself is so frequently opaque of susceptible of more than one interpretation. It is that the views of others on him are frequently either double-edged or completely unexpected.

Take, for example, Sir Roy Welensky, at the time of his closest contacts with Butler Prime Minister of the Central African Federation. Welensky was a notoriously forthright and unsubtle politician, a man whose nature was direct, rough and pioneering and who went, almost, to the extent of making a fetish of his character. He was, as Iain Macleod, whom he hated, once said, a rogue elephant. A man less likely to get on with Butler, the sophisticated academic politician, it would be hard to imagine. Moreover, although Butler started his enormously complicated and difficult task in Central Africa with the declared intention of preserving what he could of the Federation, he did know that radical change would be necessary, that the secession of Nyasaland was inevitable and that the break-up of the Federation into its component parts was at least likely, if not probable. As time went by, moreover, the necessity of dissolving the Federation became a conviction, and if not as much in Butler's mind as in that of Macmillan, it was still a general feeling among the counsels of the British government. In his memoirs *4,000 Days*, Welensky is, in general, splenetic on the subject of British politicians. But this is what he has to say of Butler:

> He has a very incisive intelligence; he seems almost glacial in his manner, but he is a man of deep feeling and almost impenetrable reserve. He is orderly, precise and quick-thinking. He is very flexible in negotiation, but when he has reached his decision he does not change it. Trying to look at the whole tragedy of the destruction of the Federation in perspective and as objectively as I can, I think that Rab Butler was the best British Minister I dealt with in the years from 1957 onwards, and he had the roughest, most unpleasant job.

And again:

> He was at all times friendly and frank and displayed

> none of the built-in prejudices to which we had become accustomed. He listened courteously; he made no easy, flattering or headline-catching promises; and he gave the same serious consideration to the opinions and feelings of the European minority as to those of the African majority. He did not give the impression that the solution to all our problems was a simple affair of head-counting.

Nor has Welensky merely written in a friendly way about Butler: he spared no pains, as the life of the Federation moved towards its close, to distinguish the Secretary of State and his wife from his colleagues. At the end of March 1963 it was clear to Welensky and his colleagues that the British government would in no circumstances seek to turn back the rising tide of black nationalism, nor even to stem it. The decision, indeed, had been taken to break up the Federation into its component parts – Southern Rhodesia (now Zimbabwe), Northern Rhodesia (now Zambia) and Nyasaland (now Malawi). On 29 March Welensky and his delegation were due to lunch with Macmillan and his colleagues and the other delegations attending the constitutional conference. Butler first saw the Federal Prime Minister, and announced to him the gist of what Her Majesty's government proposed to do: Welensky immediately cancelled his attendance at the lunch; but he continued to treat the Butlers with every measure of courtesy, friendship, and even deference. Welensky writes:

> I did not attempt at that moment to conceal my anger or my grief; but thinking it all over, I do not feel in the least harsh or bitter towards Rab Butler, I believe that had he been given a reasonable chance, the story might have been a different one.

Butler, says Welensky of this occasion, 'looked stricken', and he gives a vivid portrait of a man whose policy and ambition alike had failed. However, most British political, and subsequent scholarly opinion has it that the achievement of the dissolution of the Federation without violence constituted one of Butler's greatest triumphs, and there is little doubt that Butler himself shares that view. Yet, unlike any other British politician, he made his way straight to Welensky's heart; and Welensky was not a man easy to fool, or one likely to fall for the blandishments of even the most subtle and persuasive of British politicians. Before he came out of Africa, of course, Welensky, as he wrote, knew him and liked him. But he was also suspicious:

> But in this new appointment, with this far-reaching authority over my country's destiny, would he be friend of foe? Would he hold to principles and pledges? Or would he take the road of expediency and appeasement? Would he be just a smooth and subtle negotiator? Would he be a hatchet-man? Or, as more than one of my friends in the Federation and Britain suggested, had Mr Macmillan called him – a little prematurely perhaps – as the undertaker?

The complicated history of the wind-up of the Federation does not concern us here; nor need we seek a final judgement on the once vexed question of whether there was any serious or long-term alternative to the policy of withdrawal which Macmillan adopted (which led, in the fullness of time, to the Unilateral Declaration of Independence by Southern Rhodesia, a seven-year guerrilla war, and the birth of the independent state of Zimbabwe). What is striking is the impression made by Butler on those he negotiated with, and on the defeated Welensky in particular.

Those who lose in the kind of situation that existed in Central Africa in the early sixties are unlikely to revere those who ensured their defeat. Macleod, Duncan Sandys and the late Reginald Maudling were all, at different times, vilified by white Africa, Macleod in particular, not least because he enjoyed the esteem, and even the love, of black Africa. Butler, of course, lost further ground on the right wing of the Conservative Party as the result of the ditching of Welensky. Sandys, though he played, over the years, a much more striking role in the creation of independent Africa, neither gained anything like the same reputation among blacks as Macleod did, nor lost ground in politics at home to the extent that Butler did. And what Maudling did as Colonial Secretary was scarcely noticed either way. Butler was the one who, despite Welensky's appraisal, suffered most in the Conservative Party because of what he had done in Africa.

I have little doubt that Welensky greatly exaggerates whatever feelings of regret Butler may have had at the demise of the Federation. To be sure he may well, on taking up the job, have even had high hopes of holding things together in some way. No doubt he was, at the end, both sympathetic to Welensky and even regretful in his presence. But it is certain that Butler, surveying the contemporary African scene, and remembering his own sympathy so many years previously with the radical youth of India, would not have believed for very long or very deeply that, in British Africa at any rate, it would be possible to preserve white dominance once black nationalism was on the march. And being the progressive that he is, he not only regarded the coming hour of the blacks as inevitable but sympathized with it. But oddly enough, Welensky's favourable impression of him emerges despite all that.

Remote and impenetrable are two of the words Welensky uses to describe Butler. I have already described that conversation with Moran in which he told Churchill's doctor that Butler was easily able to bear the extraordinary strain of his own high office, and of standing in for both the Prime Minister and the Foreign Secretary at the same time, because of the exceptional peace and normality of his private life. I have also mentioned the fact that it was not until late in his political life – when he was Home Secretary – that he took to making any regular use of the House of Commons smoking room. It was not, therefore, just because of his manner and his academic interests that Butler seemed, throughout his time in politics, to be more than a little aloof from the day-to-day activities and concerns of his political colleagues. It was also that he inhabited, in addition to theirs, a quite different world, and he did so by choice, deliberately insulating himself and his family from the hurly-burly of politics – rather in the way Enoch Powell does today. Such a stance has very considerable advantages: when a busy man, especially one constantly beset by the numerous storms and unexpected eddies of politics, can come home and close the door on the world, finding tranquillity and security within, he has a definite bonus in the opportunities thus offered to recharge his batteries. But the feeling that he is not fully involved which such a mode of living can also convey can hurt him: at the two great leadership crises of 1957 and 1963 when Butler lost, he truly had only the most general idea of the sentiments of the party in the House, let alone in the country. He had no real understanding of where he was strong and where he was weak, and he did not bestir himself to find out.

The other world – the private world of R.A. Butler – was inhabited, however, by more than his family. He is one of that surprisingly large band of Conservative ministers this century who are also painters: Churchill, of course, is the most famous, though Butler himself believes that the best were Patrick Buchanan Hepburn (Chief Whip and later Lord Hailes) and Lord Alexander (Field Marshall and Minister of Defence in the 1951 government). (In our own day Lord Thorneycroft, Chairman of the Conservative Party, and Nicholas Ridley, Minister of State at the Foreign Office, are among the best of parliamentary painters, though Duncan Sandys has a good reputation in the field and there are enough contributors to mount an exhibition of members' paintings each year.) Butler began to paint at school, and recourse to brush and easel has been his main relaxation ever since, especially in times of stress. He likes, particularly, to tackle landscapes, and confesses to the belief that 'I have a certain facility with skies ...' Many of his landscapes are of the Isle of Mull where, in 1960, he and his second wife acquired a holiday home, Frachadil, where, in retirement, he has spent more and more of his time, and which he obviously loves deeply. 'I do not think', he wrote, 'that my best pictures are worse than Winston Churchill's and he did not think so either. But mine are neither so valuable nor so profuse.'

Of Churchill's painting Butler observes, 'There is little intellectual content in his work. It was thus, as it was meant to be, a complete recreation and comfort in the periods when his tumultuous career provided intermissions.' His own painting is similarly non-intellectual in character, and has served a similar purpose for him. Deprecatingly, he compares his work to the kind of framed view once seen in railway carriages, and he has never displayed it except in the private rooms of his homes. Not for him anything so brash as Churchill's submission of pictures to the Royal Academy. Though his principal relaxation, he does not take it terribly seriously.

Since painting is an activity so frequently practised by politicians it cannot be held to be one of the activities which set Butler apart from his colleagues. What is more likely to have contributed to that was his steadily deepening involvement in the world of the academic study of literature. I have already discussed the very substantial academic records of both his own family and that of the Courtaulds. During the life of the 1951 government Butler became President of the Royal Society of Literature and promptly appointed as Chairman of its Council another scion of a great political family, Lord Birkenhead. Lord

Birkenhead is, of course, a distinguished biographer and historian, mainly in the field of political history (though he has, of course, also written a fine life of Kipling). Despite, therefore, the establishment at the head of its affairs of two such predominantly politically orientated men, the Society went on to achieve great distinction in its output of material on poetry (where Butler's friend the Poet Laureate, Cecil Day Lewis, was the predominant influence) and modern literary criticism. The Butlers themselves have not been behindhand in their contributions. Lady Butler has written a distinguished essay on the more recondite and complicated aspects of Proust, and Butler himself delivered an interesting and important lecture on what is probably his favourite theme – the art of indirect autobiography, by which he means, principally, the use of the personal experience of the author in the construction of his novels.

The list of authors paraded by Butler not only in his lecture to the Royal Society of Literature on indirect autobiography, but in his Romanes Lecture, 'The difficult art of autobiography', gives a good indication of his general reading – Tolstoy (whose *War and Peace* and *Kreutzer Sonata* are his favourite examples), but also Conrad, Hemingway, Maugham, Lawrence, Dickens, George Eliot, Meredith and Proust. When I first met him in 1970, Butler was toying with the idea of a book on this subject, but inquiries over the years have elicited replies so vague that it seems unlikely that he ever got very far with it.

Surprisingly, given his background and the educational habits of the time of his youth, Butler is no great classicist. When packing books for his world tour with Sydney (before he entered politics) he included a number, in translations, of the Greek and Roman classics – Plato, Xenophon, Cicero, Demosthenes and Aristotle (with whose work he says he could never come to terms). He has a ready stock of classical quips, and uses them frequently, but one does not feel that the Greek and Latin masters are in his intellectual bloodstream as one feels, for example, of Quintin Hogg. Aside from his taste in fiction (including, rather unexpectedly, Robert Louis Stevenson), Butler's principal interest has always, and hardly surprisingly, lain in political history. Like the great Duke of Wellington he prepared himself for every task by reading up the subject generally, and by examining all the historical precedents for what he had to do. Thus, a substantial period of time on the world tour was spent on the history of British India: his reading then provided him with formidable equipment for the first task he was to undertake in government and, of course, it gave him that ambition to be Viceroy of India to which he constantly refers. One feels, however, that reading in political history has never given him the unalloyed pleasure of artistic literature: it was always principally a task, undertaken with a goodly measure of enjoyment, no doubt, but still, essentially, part of work.

It is a great pity that Butler has not found more time to tackle literary criticism. He did say, when he became Master of Trinity, that it was his intention to make up for the lost years, and to make some perhaps minor, but not insubstantial, contribution to literary scholarship. It has not turned out that way; and his principal pedagogical interest while he was Master of Trinity turned out to be a generalized and gentle supervision of the university education of the Prince of Wales, something which undoubtedly gave him great pleasure (especially when Prince Charles achieved a creditable degree) but which is hardly the stuff of serious teaching or scholarship. Thus, except on incidental occasions, and on the odd individual text, Butler's probing, allusive mind, with both its insight and its capacity for the detection of irony and ambiguity, has never been fully turned on the texts which, in other circumstances, might have made up his professional life.

When Butler, though Chancellor of the Exchequer, was also standing in for Churchill and Eden, his friend James

Stuart (Secretary of State for Scotland in the Churchill government) being, like many others, worried about the burden he was bearing, wrote to him saying, 'You seem well – and I hope you are – but do please remember that you mustn't break the main spring. It takes ages to mend.' By the time he retired altogether from politics Butler's main spring was, I believe, broken.

Given his age, and the multiple strains and responsibilities of his life – it should be remembered that he was never off his party's front bench from the moment of his first appointment to the day of his retirement – it can hardly be said to be surprising that Butler should have relaxed at Cambridge. It was not that he was not busy: he interested himself in all the college's affairs, was actively concerned with what was being done for the education of young men in one of the largest houses of the two old English universities, and paid particular attention to the quality of the food and wine emerging from Trinity's capacious kitchens and cellars. He became President of the Cambridge Conservative Association, and of the graduate Conservative Association, at whose dinners he rapidly became a familiar, slumped, lugubrious but vastly entertaining figure. If he had not frequented the smoking room during his years in the House of Commons he rapidly became – if in Cambridge – a fixture in the Trinity Fellows' Parlour after dinner each evening. And in the outside world he retained many associations, notably with literary societies and with the National Association for Mental Health, of which organization he also became President. Finally, with the aid of Peter Goldman (a former protégé at the Conservative Research Department) and Lucia Santa Cruz, daughter of the Chilean Ambassador to London, he embarked on his memoirs.

But he was not busy to any great effect. There are many in the two great universities who resent the continuation in those few institutions, where it remains, of the use of the royal prerogative in the appointment of a head. That Butler aroused very little such antagonism when he was put forward by Harold Wilson was the result of a strong feeling that here was a man who was coming home – here was no whimsical decision to make an old political cart-horse happy by giving him something to do in retirement that would amuse him. Cambridge opinion was much more positive. It was appreciated, of course, that it is always something of an advantage to have as the head of a great educational institution a man who knows the ropes and the telephone numbers of Whitehall, and Butler was certainly eminently qualified in that respect. But his reverence for scholarship was known to be so great, his family tradition was so strong, his own preferences so frequently and cogently expressed, and his ambitions in scholarly fields so frequently alluded to, that Cambridge, I believe, expected more of him than he any longer had the strength to give.

'All dignity, no power,' he once said to me of the period of his Mastership. 'I am moderately respectable,' he wrote deprecatingly of his qualifications to take up a position which was, so to speak, in the family, his great-uncle Montagu having occupied it before. But Trinity is a big place – 118 Fellows and nearly 1000 students – and one of very settled traditions. Even a reform-minded Master much younger and physically stronger than Butler (whose health began to decline not long after his appointment, and who has since suffered more than one heart attack) would have had his work cut out to change its character or its course. A younger Butler might have wanted to, but the man who came there after a life in politics and the turmoil of the public world, while he was to discharge his duties with efficiency and dedication, loved the pastures too much to want to plough them up. 'My dear Rab,' an old political friend said to him once, 'it's never totally possible to be absolutely unhappy looking out on Great Court.'

In the House of Lords Butler decided to sit on the cross benches, owing formal allegiance to no political party. As might have been expected this decision, faintly ludicrous, some thought, in a man who had served one party so loyally for so many years, gave rise to many questions. In particular, it was thought to express disapproval of changing trends within the Tory Party, and particularly its steady move away – which began after the 1964 election – from the liberal and paternalist tradition of which he was himself so much a part. Butler scouted such notions – though they were rapidly revived when, after Mrs Thatcher was elected, he joined with the Duke of Norfolk to scupper a government plan to reduce transport facilities for school children, holding it to be a breach of the spirit of his own Education Act. His argument was that it was unseemly for the Master of Trinity to be partisan in the Upper House – though that same Master did not find himself inhibited from joining fully in the political activities of his old party in the local politics of Cambridge. The extent and the vigour of his activity has, naturally, declined over the years, but for a man who had seen and done so much, and who had such good reason to feel disappointed if not embittered with the way he had been treated, he continued to give regular and sedulous attention to the public service.

It is this disposition to serve that is, I believe, at the very heart of his nature, and of greater consequence by far than his characteristics of ambiguity and ambivalence. In 1914 his uncle Geoffrey published a little book on the Conservative tradition, and it has been Butler's *vade mecum* in politics ever since: he has even produced a new edition of it. Of its many typical passages the one he chose to quote in his own memoirs reads:

> Resistance to predatory attacks upon property, and the like, will always form important items in the Tory programme. But Tory doctrine loses all that is ennobling in

> its appeal, if it confines itself to these; if it fails, that is, to get down to the principles which lie beneath all such resistance. The great Tory leaders of the past challenge us to something more, and by their challenge show us the secret of their own irresistible example. The captains of Toryism in the past can be made the instructors of Toryism in the present: and the Tory tradition is the Tory hope.

Butler comments:

> Many years later I wrote my own preface to ... the book in which I sought to identify the legacy of these captains of Toryism. What they had left us, I insisted, was not a collection of causes for which we were obliged to die in the last ditch, nor a set of premises by whose consistent application we might infallibly regulate our conduct, but a mature tradition of political thought and behaviour which is neither fixed nor finished. This tradition at its best is responsible to the demands of each new age, empirical as to method, resourceful in expressing itself in popular idiom, though deeply conscious that the 'councils to which Time is not called, Time will not ratify'.

Now this is all both elevated and elevating. The great difficulty about it is to discern with any precision what it means in practical political circumstances. It is the kind of general view the real nature of which can truly be understood only in its application to specific circumstances. Thus, it is easy to look back over Butler's long career and demonstrate that on every major issue which came his way he was in the van of enlightened, progressive or, to choose a more concrete word, reformist opinion. But many of these issues (India, for example) can be of historical interest only, while in the case of others – and especially, perhaps, his educational reforms, stoutly though he blames what has gone wrong on those who succeeded him – perspectives and judgements have changed. Certainly he is regarded with, if anything, greater suspicion and, occasionally, dislike from among ranks of the modern Conservative Party than he ever was by the party in which he grew up and achieved prominence. And with the best will in the world, even when one reads such admirers of his as Mr Henry Fairlie, it is not easy to understand and appreciate the force of Butlerism, nor the passion which it commanded and which, though in smaller circles nowadays, it still commands. The short term – the long term may and, I believe, will, show a more positive response – has not been kind to the Butler heritage.

It should, of course, be pointed out that the decline of Butler's influence did not begin with his retirement. Even the Home Office had been something of a backwater for him, and his real collapse began after he was beaten to the post by Lord Home. Because of the shortness of his time as Prime Minister and leader it is too little appreciated how sweeping were the changes introduced in the Conservative Party by Home: the paradox is that the fourteenth Earl, whose elevation was taken in so many quarters to symbolize how irredeemably reactionary his party was, in fact prepared the ground for the entry into full power of the new Tories, non- or even anti-aristocratic, of a lower social class than the Butlers and the Macmillans, unashamedly meritocratic, and far less burdened by the responsibilities and traditions of paternalistic Toryism than were Macmillan, Butler, or for that matter, Home himself. Lord Home made the path clear for Edward Heath and Margaret Thatcher.

When the leadership changed in 1963 the whole top storey of the party's establishment changed too. Macleod refused to serve, as did Lord Aldington. The new Chairman of the party was John Hare, ennobled as Lord Blakenham.

But not one of the three previous chairmen of the party – Hogg, Butler and Macleod – had any further influence on its immediate development of policy save such as they enjoyed as departmental ministers. It is true that Butler continued, under Home, as Chairman of the Advisory Committee on Policy, a rather strange body which owed its ultimate origins to his own Committee on Post-war Problems, and which was supposed to encourage and facilitate liaison between the government, the party and the National Union (the umbrella body of local Conservative organizations). But the fact is that he could easily remain as Chairman because the job was becoming increasingly unimportant, increasingly far from the centre of things. It was originally supposed to process and approve major statements on policy, and did so, for example, in the case of *Onward in Freedom* in 1958. The committee's decline may be demonstrated by the fact that when Macmillan came to present the argument for the most significant change in post-war Conservative policy – the decision to apply for membership of the European Economic Community – he did so in a pamphlet, *Britain, the Commonwealth and Europe*, signed by himself and published by Central Office. Thus, though the machinery through which Butler had produced the great post-1945 developments in policy remained in existence, atrophy had taken place before his own withdrawal to Cambridge. Thereafter Edward du Cann, the party Chairman appointed by Home, and subsequently the new leader, Edward Heath, made policy in quite a different way. Heath (who quarrelled with and dismissed du Cann) favoured the making of policy through the creation of a vast complex of policy groups frequently drawing their main strength from outside the party altogether. Margaret Thatcher, when, in turn, she succeeded Heath, preferred to carry on policy formulation through the medium of backbench committees – not least because she inherited a parliamentary party considerably disillusioned with what it took to be Heath's contempt for its processes. The precise and delicate balance which Butler had created after the war was never to reappear.

It is no secret that Butler in retirement has been far from happy about the direction taken by the party which in its modern guise he did so much to mould. As I described earlier, the success of Butler's post-war work depended very much on Churchill's tolerance of his activities, and if it was extremely difficult and trying at times to obtain the great man's specific approval for specific policies it was none the less the case that the leader's benevolent attitude to his labours was vitally important in getting his ideas and message through. Part of his disillusionment after 1964 has, I think, lain in the fact that the broadening of responsibility or policy outwards from the leader, which he believed to be an important part of the evolution of the Conservative Party, has now been arrested: the very profusion of committees and *ad hoc* advisory bodies has meant that, in practice, the leader has gained in strength and authority at the expense of the party machinery. It has not, of course, helped that the leaders the party has chosen since Home have led it in a policy direction by no means to Butler's liking. It is true that now (in 1981) Edward Heath is advocating a kind of Toryism not unlike Butler's. But it was Heath's shake-up of the party in the second half of the sixties that constituted the main break with the post-war tradition. Though Heath eventually failed and changed his policies, the strength he had enabled the New Right (so-called to distinguish them from the old, paternalistic and imperialistic right, and vastly more concerned with strict economic policy than the Old Right ever were) to seize, meant that when the time came to overthrow him they were able to organize effectively around a leader, Mrs Thatcher, who more truly represented their ideas. To nearly all the developments – and especially those in economic policy – that Mrs Thatcher has brought about

Butler is opposed (like Macmillan in this if nothing else), though his personal regard for the Prime Minister is quite as high as Macmillan's own.

It follows that, enfeebled though his position by then was, the period between 1963 and the general election of 1964 was the last in which the ideas Butler had brought forward after the war, and which constitute the essence of his political heritage, were heard on the national stage, and in relation not just to general attitudes, but specifically to policy and the work of the government. It is true that he had only recently been associated with a measure – for the control of immigration from the Commonwealth – which the more enthusiastic and devoted of his followers viewed with concern, if not dismay. Butler expressed some of their feeling when he introduced the Bill in November 1961, saying that the government had decided to act 'only after long and anxious consideration and a considerable reluctance. Given', he added, 'a too rapid increase in the number of immigrants, there is a real risk that the drive for improved conditions will be defeated by the sheer weight of numbers.' This defence of his legislation based specifically and unrelentingly on the argument that control was necessary to amelioration is the quintessential liberal Butler: one could never imagine him saying – as Enoch Powell and Margaret Thatcher have said subsequently – that control of immigration could be justified by the simple resentment of the native Briton against a foreign influx. The principle must always relate to humanitarian good, and that relationship is the golden thread of Butler's political philosophy.

The fact remains that, at the Home Office, Butler had been pushed much further to the right than he cared to be, something which is often the fate of Home Secretaries of either party. I have already discussed the sheer horror which visited him when he had to consider whether a criminal sentenced to death should or should not be reprieved. And it is possible to detect an almost querulously defensive note in a speech in October 1961 denying that the appeal authorities were too lenient in their paroling of those sentenced to life imprisonment:

> There has been a sort of idea that nine years is the usual term of life imprisonment. That is, of course, not so. Those released from life sentence in recent years have included men detained for much longer periods, up to twenty years. Many men must be, and have been, kept in for life. All life sentence prisoners are released on licence and can be recalled to prison by the Secretary of State at any time if this is thought desirable.

Privately, however, Butler was quite clear in his mind that the more stentorian tones, not only of public opinion, but of his party, were mistaken. This did not mean he could not be partisan. In 1963 he tried to set out his ideal of democracy – and against the political background of a Labour Party not just hungry for power but seeking it with effectiveness:

> What the theory of democracy *does* say is that the electorate should be able to make at each election a sensible choice between alternative policies. Those who believe in democracy, as we do, believe that, whatever the aberrations of individual judgement, the general collective wisdom of the community can thus get closest to the best form of government. We accept this as the reason for democracy. What nonsense it is then to accept as inevitable and right the so-called swing of the pendulum. If we accept uncritically the theory of 'it's time for a change' – still more if we regard government as a sort of cricket match, when each side must have its innings in turn – then we may be condemned for ever to an alternation between sensible and silly policies. After all, if the sillies can always be sure of re-election if they wait

> long enough, then there is no compulsion on them to make themselves sensible.

That passage is clear, it is coherent, and it is sensible. The difficulty about it, from Butler's point of view, is that it was delivered to the Conservative Party Conference in Blackpool just at the moment – Macmillan having announced his resignation – when it was important to sound a tocsin. Yet, calmly, deliberately, with the slightly impatient aid of his wife, Butler decided not to bang the drums. His idea – his ideal – of service, though it encompassed putting plans and policies in a reasonably popular form, did not include going all out for R. A. Butler. He had (and, I think, has) no conception of how much his decision not to fight meant to people like Macleod, Powell and Aldington, not to mention many much humbler party servitors. He did his duty as a retainer of the nation exactly as he saw it. He did that duty – again, as he saw it – throughout his long and complex career. He saw no higher good. This biographer, who has less than full sympathy with the views and policies that Lord Butler has stood for, must, however, bend in admiration for his steadfastness; and even wish that the charge of the country, at a crucial point in its life, had been put in his less than flashy hands.